THE ADHD PRODUCTIVITY MANUAL

PRAISE FOR *THE ADHD PRODUCTIVITY MANUAL*

"I'm a season ticket holder for all things produced by Ari Tuckman. His masterful new book, The ADHD Productivity Manual, is his best work yet. In an ADHD-friendly manner, Dr. Tuckman has crystallized what you need to know and more importantly do and how to do it in this incomparable guide for living well with ADHD. This book will undoubtedly improve lives, including yours!"

– J. Russell Ramsay, Ph.D., ABPP, psychologist and author of The Adult ADHD Toolkit, Rethinking Adult ADHD, and The Adult ADHD & Anxiety Workbook

"Ari Tuckman has done it again. The ADHD Productivity Manual is practical, empowering, and refreshingly honest. He gives ADHD adults exactly what we need: zero BS strategies and deep respect. The reflection questions at the end of each chapter invite real transformation. This book will help you be more productive — but more importantly, it'll help you live a good life."

– Kristen Carder, Certified Coach, Host of the I Have ADHD Podcast, Founder of FOCUSED ADHD Coaching

"This is the closest thing I've seen to a comprehensive owner's manual for your ADHD brain. And like a good owner's manual, it's compact, to-the-point, and full of actionable 'troubleshooting' prompts/solutions. Use it as a step-by-step guide, or as an a la carte menu depending on your particular challenge du jour. Either way, one of the best minds in the ADHD solutions arena has provided perhaps the ultimate roadmap to more traction and less frustration in your ADHD life."

– Alan P. Brown, ADHD Coach and Creator of ADD Crusher™

"Ari Tuckman has done it again! With his trademark humor and compassionate candor, Ari walks us through our ADHD struggles with wisdom and grace, uplifting us with this inspiring, powerful, and practical guide to our own success."

– Nachi Felt, PhD, Adjunct Professor of Psychology and Education, Co-Director of the Cognition and Neuroscience Lab at Teachers College, Columbia University

"Ari Tuckman PsyD gets it. In The ADHD Productivity Manual, he delivers the perfect mix of validation, insight, and practical tools for people with ADHD who want to get things done—and feel good about themselves in the process. Dr. Tuckman's humor, honesty, and deep clinical experience shine through in every chapter. This isn't just a book about productivity—it's a guide to building a better life with ADHD, one doable step at a time."

– Stephanie Moulton Sarkis, PhD, author and psychotherapist www.stephaniesarkis.com

"The search is over for a hands-on, practical, compassionate guide on increasing productivity for individuals (like myself) living with ADHD. Many workbooks out there talk the talk but Dr. Ari Tuckman actually delivers, to an audience he has advocated for and treated for over 25 years! He takes the common obstacles and overwhelming challenges those with ADHD know all too well and makes it less scary and, dare I say it, even fun to tackle. He possesses a wealth of information and more importantly translates that knowledge into strategies that someone with ADHD would realistically use. The tone of the book, like Dr. Tuckman, is educative, validating and encouraging—with a sense of humor sprinkled throughout the pages."

– Roberto Olivardia, Ph.D., Clinical Psychologist, Lecturer in the Department of Psychiatry, Harvard Medical School. Parent of two college students with ADHD.

"Imagine managing your life -- seriously, handling all the necessary details -- without falling into a constant ADHD shame cycle? Tuckman's ADHD Productivity Manual strikes a balance so you can manage your mindset to get things done!"

– Elaine Taylor-Klaus, MCC, CEO ImpactParents.com, Author of The Essential Guide to Raising Complex Kids with ADHD, anxiety, and more and Parenting ADHD Now! Easy Intervention Strategies to Empower Kids with ADHD

"In his terrific new book, The ADHD Productivity Manual, Dr. Ari Tuckman offers a smart, practical guide to living a better life with ADHD. It feels like having a conversation with a kind and knowledgeable therapist ally who really wants to guide you in showing up, improving your performance and noticing your successes along the way. I really love this book and I will definitely recommend it to my clients, friends and community!"

– Sharon Saline, PhD, Author of What Your ADHD Child Wishes You Knew: Working Together to Empower Kids for Success in School and Life and The ADHD Solution Card Deck

"With practical compassionate advice, Dr. Tuckman shares deep insight into why people with ADHD struggle with productivity and how to move forward. He offers a vital and easy to follow guide for anyone looking to get ahead of their ADHD and more easily keep up with the demands of everyday life."

– Mark Bertin, MD, Author of Mindful Parenting for ADHD and Mindfulness and Self Compassion for Teen ADHD

ABOUT THE AUTHOR

Ari Tuckman, PsyD, MBA is a psychologist, international presenter, and ADHD thought leader. He is the author of five books on adult ADHD. He is widely respected for his insight, humor, and commitment to improving the lives of those with ADHD and those who love them.

He has given more than 750 presentations and podcast interviews and routinely earns excellent reviews for his ability to make complicated information understandable and useful. He serves as a co-chair of CHADD's conference committee and was awarded the 2023 Hall of Fame award for his significant contributions to the field. A popular expert and advocate, he has been widely quoted in national media and serves as an expert for Understood.org. He is in private practice in West Chester, PA.

OTHER BOOKS BY ARI TUCKMAN

ADHD After Dark: Better Sex Life, Better Relationship

Understand Your Brain, Get More Done: The ADHD Executive Functions Workbook

More Attention, Less Deficit: Success Strategies for Adults with ADHD

Integrative Treatment for Adult ADHD: A Practical, Easy-to-Use Guide for Clinicians

ABOUT THE ILLUSTRATOR

Marcy Caldwell, Psy.D., is a clinical psychologist, writer, and speaker who bridges her clinical expertise with visual storytelling to champion those with neurodiverse brains. As the owner and director of The Center for ADHD and founder of ADDept.org, she is dedicated to helping people craft systems and environments that highlight their strengths and minimize their struggles. A nationally recognized speaker featured in top outlets like The New York Times and a consultant to Fortune 500 companies, Dr. Marcy is equally inspired by research and her own vibrant family full of neurodiversity, where creativity and curiosity spark a love of adventure and understanding.

The ADHD Productivity Manual

Ari Tuckman, PsyD, MBA

Working Memory Press
West Chester, PA

ISBN-13: 979-8-9985784-0-3 (Paperback)
ISBN-13: 979-8-9985784-1-0 (eBook)

Library of Congress Control Number: 2025908845

For Bailey. You're one of the most productive people I know. More importantly, you're always curious about how things work and willing to figure out when they don't.

CONTENTS

ACKNOWLEDGEMENTS

It's important to have great people in your life.

Marcy Caldwell, PsyD took my simple ideas for illustrations and made them look even better than I could have hoped.

The world of ADHD is full of amazing people doing really cool stuff. I would like to thank Christine Hargrove, Stephanie Sarkis, Mike Felt, Kristen Carder, Roberto Olivardia, Alan Brown, Sara Markowitz, and Jessica McCabe for offering suggestions on the manuscript and making this a much better book. These folks are the best of the ADHD community.

Shawndra Holmberg guided me through the self-publishing process with a steady hand. It's been a pleasure. I look forward to doing it again. I keep saying that my next book will be about ADHD and self-esteem, so hopefully this time I mean it.

In her role as editor, Anne Holmberg tightened up and clarified my writing without changing my voice. She also told me which jokes didn't work, so you owe her for that, too.

Jason Anscomb created exactly the cover I was hoping for. Collaborating with him was a joy.

INTRODUCTION:
SERIOUSLY, ANOTHER ADHD BOOK?

YOU HOLD IN YOUR HAND not a book, but a hope—a brave hope that this time will be different, that this book will contain strategies that will last longer than the bananas you forgot to buy. Sure, every strategy is interesting the first time you use it. A few are even interesting the third time. And if you used them at the right time and place then that's bonus points.

The aim of this book is to fill in all those gaps—all those places where the right strategy evades you but, sadly, the consequences don't. That consequence might be the meeting where everyone knew you weren't prepared. Or the consequence may be the potentially disastrous situation that you scrambled to rescue so no one's the wiser. But you know what happened (and can't stop thinking about it).

The obvious goal of this book is to help you get more done. The less obvious, but more important goal is that I want you to feel good about yourself. It's easy to feel good about yourself when you hit all the marks, but we all blow it sometimes. We also need to feel good about ourselves when things don't go according to plan. Or there wasn't actually a plan which, it turns out, would have been helpful. And, since you probably don't live on an island by yourself, you need to know how to manage others' expectations so that everyone is happier with the end result.

We're going to talk a lot about ADHD and productivity, but really, this book is about living a good life. This means having the time and energy to not only check off all the boring stuff, but to actually have time to pursue what is interesting and meaningful. These lost opportunities are the ultimate price of not managing your ADHD well. So, write this on your hand: "I want to live a good life." That's really what we're doing here.

Yes, It Will Be Difficult

So this is a terrible way to get a reader psyched about a book, but here's the blunt truth: Almost every single thing I suggest in this book will be hard to do. Or at least a stretch. Partly this is because you're already doing all the easy stuff. Also, you've already figured out a bunch of hard stuff that you keep doing because it works (and has probably gotten easier with practice). This book is going to fill in around what you're already doing. If someone tells you that managing ADHD or behavior change in general is easy, then they're selling you something—that won't help. You deserve better than another setup and then another disappointment.

> Willpower is important, but it's never enough.

Part of what you're fighting here is human nature—we all make mistakes, we all forget things, we all optimistically talk ourselves into shortcuts. You're also fighting the tide of your ADHD and how it can pull you around. It's easy to let your days flow and just go where they take you, but to fight the tide, you need to put in the effort—from moment to moment, day to day, and year to year. It's tiring, but that's where the real rewards are. So, part of what we're going to talk about is figuring out what will make that effort feel worthwhile, because that's where the motivation is going to come from.

Here's another blunt truth—there are a thousand things that can impact your productivity. There's no such thing as the seven hacks that are going to supercharge your... whatever. From moment to moment, there are all sorts of things that can impact whether you get something done or don't. I'm going to cover a lot of them. Your job is to figure out which are the ones that are most relevant for you. On the plus side, you get to skip the pages that don't seem as relevant, at least for now.

Why This Book Is Different

I spend most of my time working with clients, most of whom have ADHD. We talk about all the usual therapy topics, but probably talk more about productivity than most other therapists and clients. Over twenty-five years of full-time practice, I've done more than 40,000 client hours. You learn a few things over that time. It taught me what works and what doesn't, that people are complicated, and that what worked today may not work tomorrow, so there are no one-size-fits-all solutions. And also, there are very few "transformative," "revolutionary," or "life changing" ideas out there—it's great for marketing, but seriously, what are the odds that some rando discovered something that powerful that no one else ever did?

I take my responsibility as a therapist really seriously. People come to me because they're suffering and they deserve my best efforts. Same goes for my readers and presentation audiences, too. This book represents everything I've learned about how to help people (mostly with ADHD) be more productive, broken down into accessible, practical, ADHD-friendly chunks.

How to Use This Book

There is a rationale for the order of the chapters, but you can also jump ahead to the section that will be most helpful today. If your romantic partner then notices that you're already, like, fifty pages in, just nod and smile.

Just keep showing up and trying new things. Oh, and expect to suck at things the first time you try them—we usually do. That's the way it's supposed to be. The only way to be good at something is to keep doing it.

The point here isn't to get through the book as quickly as possible. There's no book report due tomorrow. Or yesterday. Take your time to really think about these ideas. Is this relevant for you? Where, how and in what situations? If not, why not? If it used to be but isn't now, what did you learn to manage it better?

Write all over this book. Highlight the good parts. Cross out the junk. Scribble notes. Yell at the pages or to the heavens. Quote lines to your friends but act as if you just thought of it.

From the Page to Your Life

Ideas are interesting, but what's more interesting is making your life better. The goal is to take these ideas and apply them into your life, put them to work, and then reap the benefits. I say that ADHD is a disorder of converting intentions into actions. This book is all about action. The good news is that you will spend less time reading and more time doing. The other good news (hopefully!) is that you get to do a bunch of stuff. Think of it as a field trip for your brain. And the best part is that you don't need to be perfect—just a bit better, a bit more often.

That feels doable.

In addition to all the strategies, each chapter ends with three specific tasks that will take the ideas from the page and into your life. I then give you some space to think about and write out what you are going to work on so you can make it real. Take these exercises seriously and really put in the effort to see what you can do with them. If my suggestions don't quite fit your situation, then adapt them to something better—but still put in the effort. Just like ADHD, this book is not about knowing, it's about doing. So let's talk about ways to help you do it. Then keep doing it.

Free PDF of All Put It to Work Questions

To make it easier to write your answers to all of the questions in Getting Started, Put It to Work, and the final chapter, you can download the PDF at https://adultadhdbook.com/the-adhd-productivity-manual-pdf. Yep, 128 unique questions spread out over 85 pages, so get ready to do some serious thinking. This book is all about making real changes and getting things done.

Put It to Work

- Make it real

    o Make a commitment to apply these lessons in your daily life (don't worry, I will also talk about how to stick with strategies)

    o Remind yourself that habit change comes from effort, not just awareness

    o Remind yourself that lasting change comes from persistence, from doing it again and again—and then doing it some more after you take a break from doing it (it happens)

- Capture your realizations, thoughts, activities, stumbles, saves, progress...

    o Use a journal, your phone, or by scribbling in the margins here

    o Then go back occasionally to see what you've done (and give yourself a high five)

- Just keep showing up

    o Make today a good day, regardless of what happened yesterday—what helpful thing can you do now?

    o This book is supposed to make you feel better about yourself and more optimistic about your future, so keep reminding yourself of that if you start to get down on yourself (don't worry, we'll talk about this, too)

GETTING STARTED

B EFORE WE START SLINGING STRATEGIES, let's take a second to figure out what you're doing here. Being more productive is an easy goal to endorse—hell, who wouldn't want to be more productive? If consistent and predictable productivity has felt frustratingly elusive, then it's even easier to hope for. Obviously. Even so, let's figure out why being more productive matters—to you, at this moment in your life.

Getting this really clear will affect how you approach the book and what you get out of it—and how you feel about yourself after. I'm definitely not going to say that any particular reasons are right or wrong, or good or bad. Or even better or worse. This is a matter of personal preference so objective standards don't apply. Rather, what is more helpful is to look at how likely you will be to pull it off and how you will feel about it afterwards. For example, if you would like to be more productive in less time at work so you have more time for your personal life, you should be able to make that happen, and you will probably be happy about it. On the other hand, if you're hoping to learn how to be productive enough so that you no longer have ADHD and therefore don't have to feel defective... well, that's probably not going to work out. (Nor does it have to.)

Here are some of the broad categories of potential reasons to want to be more productive:

- **More time for other goals**.

  Being more effective and efficient in what you need to do can give you more time for what you want to do. This could be time with family and friends, hobbies, personal projects, self-care (sleep, diet, exercise), or just time to veg out.

- **Tangible or financial benefits**.

  Being more productive might get you a raise at work or make you more money if you work for yourself. Or maybe it helps you complete a degree or other training that then gives you access to better opportunities.

- **More confidence**.

  If you feel bad about yourself because you too often fall short of what you expect yourself to be able to do, then improving your batting average might plug the hole that your self-esteem leaks out of. Or maybe just knowing that you're working hard at it will give you a boost.

- **Better social standing**.

  Other people expect us to do certain things and probably at certain times. This could be your kids, romantic partner, friends, coworkers, the electric company, etc. Disappointing those expectations can lead to conflict, criticism, or even the ending of the relationship—all of which we want less of.

Do any of these jump out at you more than the others? Any burning needs in that humble bullet list? They probably all resonate to some degree, but you may want to put more energy into some than others. This will be really helpful to know as you work your way through the book. Hard work is admirable and all, but the right work is even better.

Before you run out to buy an inspirational poster related to your top reason, let's look at the potential dark side. These are all reasonable hopes—but only to a point. As with everything in life, they don't work out as well when they're taken too far. So, here's how to keep each of those above reasons in the happy middle:

- **More time for other goals.**

  As much as we may value these other goals, we still need to allow ourselves to enjoy them when we have the opportunity. This means tempering that drive to always do more—and feel guilty when we're not. It also means sometimes pushing ourselves to actually do what we say we want more of—e.g., to truly connect with the people in our life rather than hide in our phone, which may feel mentally easier. Having the time is a good start, but then we need to use that time well, which often is harder than we think it should be.

- **Tangible or financial benefits.**

  More money can make your life better, but only up to a certain point. Opportunities that make your life better in some ways may come with other downsides. It's really about finding the right balance of everything in your life at that point in time. Unfortunately, different parts of our lives often compete for the same finite resources of time and attention, so we may feel like we're always torn. (This is why work/life balance is a concept.) As we move through different stages of life, these balances may shift back and forth as we prioritize different goals. An interesting life usually involves holding some tension between the different parts of our life and accepting that we need to actively manage how we divide up our time and attention.

- **More confidence.**

  I'm all in favor of strategies that help people be more effective, but that will only build your self-esteem to a certain point. The goal here isn't to

8

make you invincible or to "cure" your ADHD. You're still a fallible human. Real happiness may require raising your level of performance in certain areas but also valuing the rest of who you are. This means accepting that certain areas will continue to be a struggle, while recognizing that you are working on it. Life can still be pretty good even without you being amazing at everything. This also means learning to be happy with the progress you've made rather than setting yourself up for discouragement by repeatedly raising the bar on your desired level of performance.

- **Better social standing**.

  If your level of performance is below what you need it to be to accomplish what you want, then it's probably worth the effort to improve it—for example, reducing the number of issues that fall through the cracks so you can show your boss that you're ready for those more interesting projects. Sure, except that someone else's impressions of you also depend on their expectations and how they interpret what you do (e.g., do they notice your extra effort or the times when you drop the ball?). You can try to manage your reputation, but there may come a point where you decide that it isn't worth trying to meet someone else's standards and that you can tolerate the price that comes with that. Others' opinions can be disappointingly stuck, so sometimes we need to be OK with letting go of what others think.

As I said before, none of this is right or wrong. It's really a matter of making a well-thought-out and well-informed decision about where you are in your life now, where you want to be, and what's worth all of this time and effort. Then being willing to shift what you're doing as circumstances evolve.

So, take a few minutes to think about why you want to be more productive. Then take a few more minutes. Then think about it again tomorrow.

Consider these questions:

How do your past struggles with productivity influence how you feel about yourself now? About your ability to be more productive?

What does it mean to you to be more productive? Or less?

What have you been told (explicitly and implicitly) about your level of productivity?

How did getting diagnosed with ADHD change how you understand and feel about yourself?

How would your life be different in tangible or visible ways if you were more productive?

What about in more intangible ways, like how you would feel about yourself?

If you were really honest about why you want to be more productive, what would you not want to admit to anyone else?

What are you hoping to get from this book?

What are you willing to put into those goals for this book?

The answers to these questions will not only target your efforts, but will also be the motivation to apply yourself when you don't feel like it, when change is hard. Good ideas are fine, but the real point here is to make your life better. So, keep these reasons in the front of your mind as you plow through the rest of these pages. Maybe bookmark this page and come back to it when you're feeling frustrated or bored.

OK, now go out and buy that inspirational poster.

SECTION I. WHY DOES ADHD MAKE PRODUCTIVITY HARDER?

S UFFICE TO SAY, IF YOU'RE reading this book it's because you already know that ADHD makes productivity harder—in lots of small, large, frustrating, confusing, disappointing, embarrassing, and/or maddening ways. Sure, but *why*? As in, how exactly does ADHD influence how you do things?

The better you understand the whys of something, the more you can do something about it—not just in standard situations with premade solutions, but also in those random situations where you need to get creative. My goal for this book is to give you not just a long list of strategies (boring), but rather a framework to understand how to tackle whatever life brings. This section lays that foundation for everything that follows, so it's worth spending some time here, even though you really want to skip ahead. I promise I'll make it worth your while and throw in enough jokes to make the trip more enjoyable. But go pee first before we really get going.

GOAL

ADHD

YOU ARE HERE

1. ADHD Is All About Doing

RUSSELL BARKLEY, PHD HAS A famous quote that ADHD is not a disorder of knowing what to do; it's a disorder of doing what you know. Definitely. I sometimes say that ADHD is a disorder of reliably converting intentions (inside your head) into actions (out in the world, at the right time and place). It impacts your ability to apply your abilities to the demands of the moment. Not that anyone is perfect, but folks with ADHD have more of those distracted, forgetful, impulsive moments than others do.

Everyone gets distracted sometimes, misplaces their keys, procrastinates, loses track of time, forgets to do something, or blurts out something that may be true but was probably better left unsaid (you know, on account of that true part). We all get some free passes where life kind of moves on. Whatever.

Unfortunately, those frustrating ADHD moments use up those free passes faster than you earn them back, so it's harder to keep moving forward and still feel good about yourself. Often other people will notice those moments, but even if they don't, you still do. Here we go again...

In some basic ways, ADHD impacts many fundamental productivity skills:

- Paying attention to all the boring stuff that life requires
- Keeping track of the details of a task
- Remembering what needs to be done and when
- Organizing the necessary items and ideas
- Predicting how long a task will take, tracking time, being on time, finishing on time
- Holding back impulsive actions, including switching to a more interesting task
- Getting back on track after interruptions
- Wrapping up all the details after the novelty has worn off

All of this can be visible to others who not only notice, but then also have thoughts and feelings about it—and about you. Usually, we look at what people do and how they do it and make assumptions about the person's intentions and how they feel about the task. Given enough data points, we start to make assumptions about their character—which can carry some real consequences.

Most of the time, when we make these inferences about others based on their actions, we tend to get it right enough for society to function. But sometimes we get it totally wrong. Unfortunately, this is where ADHD makes dealing with other people messy. Remember my line that ADHD makes it harder to reliably convert intentions into actions? Well, people look at your actions and then make (inaccurate) assumptions about your intentions—and ultimately your character. This can definitely cast a long shadow on how others treat you when it comes to getting things done—which then influences how you think about yourself and how you approach tasks. It all gets psychological and messy. But fear not—we will address this too in the pages that follow.

You Need the Right Strategies

I'm sure you've tried all sorts of strategies to be more productive. And also strategies to manage the social fallout of those unproductive times. Generic good advice has a certain logical appeal to it, but unfortunately our actions tend to not be 100% logical, especially with ADHD, so presumably helpful advice isn't always helpful enough. And sometimes the advice isn't helpful at all, like leaving earlier as a solution for chronic lateness only works if you're good at noticing that it's now time to leave. And know where your keys are.

Sometimes the problem is that one good idea, by itself, isn't enough. It depends on what else is happening around us and inside us. This not only makes our performance variable, but also frustratingly unpredictable—it worked last time, so why didn't it work this time?! Again, this is true for all people who aren't robots but it is *especially* true for folks with ADHD. Adding insult to injury, this variability means that the times when you did do what was

> Quick fixes fail quickly. Meaningful change takes effort and time.

expected ended up pouring salt in the wounds of the times when you somehow didn't because they proved that you can indeed do it... at least sometimes.

The good news is that there are a whole bunch of points of intervention where you can begin to close the gap between your intentions and actions. It's also why this book isn't just a two-minute video with the top seven strategies that will dominate your ADHD or something. The question when you're feeling stuck is, what *exactly* is getting in your way here? The better you know yourself and how your brain works, the more likely it will be that you can pull enough of the right levers to get the wheels turning. It all adds up. The goal is to pull as many of those levers as you can.

As much as I would love to promise that this book will solve all your problems, ADHD-related or otherwise, the truth is that it won't. It will make some things better and will help you feel more OK with the habits or situations that don't change that much. To this end, we will seriously think about how productive you really need to be—and at what cost. We will also think about how you want to handle other people's expectations and reactions to your productivity or lack thereof—again, at what cost.

As I said in the intro, the real goal of this book is to make your life better. Being more productive is a means to an end. One of the benefits of learning to become more productive is that it gives you a greater sense of agency and a more positive self-image. Those make life better, too, especially if your ADHD has put a bunch of dents and scratches in your agency and self-image over the years. We have some big goals here, but I think that between us, we can do it.

Put It to Work

- Notice how your ADHD gets in the way of doing what you know. (This one is probably way easier than you would hope it to be which is obviously why you're reading this book.) But, since people struggle to do things for a lot of reasons, also notice when it isn't your ADHD.

- Notice how other people also have absent-minded moments, procrastinate, show up late, etc. How do they handle it? How do others? What is a reasonable level of forgiveness?

- Apply an ADHD-friendly strategy that you already know and notice how it's helpful. How does it help you convert your intention into action? How does it help you do the right thing at the right time? How can you tweak it to maybe make it a little more likely to work?

2. ADHD Makes It Harder to See Time

WHEN YOU REALLY GET DOWN to it, ADHD is all about time. It impacts your ability to manage time efficiently and get tasks done at the right time and place. When you get distracted, your attention gets hijacked by something that may be interesting in the moment but isn't the best use of your time *now* because it won't benefit you enough in the *future* (which is where the consequences show up). In this chapter and the next, I will lay out my current conceptualization of ADHD, which then sets the foundation for most of the strategies in the rest of the book. There won't be a quiz, but it will be helpful to understand.

Time Is Slippery with ADHD

One of the most important abilities humans possess is the awareness of how the past brought us to the present and then flows into the future. It allows us to apply the lessons of the past to not only today's challenges, but also to think ahead to what tomorrow might bring so we can act now to hopefully create more desirable outcomes. This allows us to actively shape our destinies rather than simply reacting to whatever is happening right now. When we talk about time management, really what we're talking about is being able to take time into account when planning our actions—doing the right things at the right times, with an eye towards future benefits and costs. This has a profound effect on our ability to create the life that we want—academically, professionally, and personally. The better we see time and act accordingly, the more influence we have.

As with all human abilities, people fall on a bell curve when it comes to being aware of time and using it to guide their actions. Some people's internal clock ticks loudly, so they're very aware of time and what they need to do when. Others' clocks tick softly, so time too often slips by unnoticed—until they suddenly notice it again. As in, "Oh my god! I have to leave!" or, "Is that due *tomorrow*?!" I'll let you guess which end of the bell curve folks with ADHD tend to hang out in. I'll also give you a moment to realize how many ADHD-friendly strategies and tools relate to tracking time and setting up future outcomes to have a bigger effect on current actions.

> **Those who don't see time well will often trip over it.**

When we talk about time management, we often treat it as one skill, but it's really a bunch of sub-abilities, such as:

- Setting priorities among competing options (what gets done first, second... last, never)

- Predicting how long an activity will take

- Creating an order for various activities, taking time restrictions into account

- Monitoring the passage of time

- Noticing the approach and arrival of a specific time

- Re-adjusting priorities and activities in relation to time as circumstances change—speed up, reduce quality/completeness, change course, etc.

Most of these should look pretty familiar. You may be better at some and struggle more with others. You may also notice that managing time well means doing at least some of these things in most moments—which kind of explains why it's so hard to do, especially when life is busy, stressful, and complicated. Or how doing these things 90% of the time can be messed up by that other 10%—I've had clients drive early to an appointment but still be late because they lost track of time in the parking lot, which is really demoralizing.

> Time flies when you're... wait, what was I supposed to be doing?

Time can feel much more slippery when you have ADHD. It's harder to keep a firm grip on it and use it well. Boring tasks feel like they take forever ("Ugh, it's only been seven minutes?") but exciting activities fly by ("Has it really been two hours already?!"). It's been said that people with ADHD suffer from *time blindness*, that they don't see time as clearly. This variability in the subjective sense of time makes predicting how long you've been doing something feel like measuring length with a stretched out, warped ruler where you don't know which inches are short and which are long. To keep track of time you need to know if it was a stretched out boring minute or a compressed exciting minute. And what's the exchange rate, anyway?

This variability can then make planning feel like wishful thinking since it can be so hard to predict how much will get done in the next chunk of time. To make it worse, any given task may involve a bunch of sub-tasks that potentially add other chunks of time:

- The time to fire up your motivation and actually start working (c'mon brain, you can do it!)

- The time needed to find the necessary items or information (which could take way longer than the task itself)

- The additional time spent taking breaks, getting distracted, managing interruptions, getting back to work, etc.

- The time spent on related tasks that aren't mission critical but are probably more fun or less boring (such as researching local attractions rather than booking the hotel)

- The time spent actually working (the pure, truly focused time)

In general, the longer a task takes, the more likely that additional time needs to be factored in and that there is a wider range of how long you might need. It also means that your productivity in this moment is more influenced by what you did or didn't do before, like whether you flagged that email that had all the required information.

All of this variability and unpredictability can make it feel like what's the point of planning, anyway? Good time management requires constant units, but it's anybody's guess how long the task will take this time. If you're totally dialed in, you might set a land speed record for how quickly you get it done. But if you just can't lock in, you may feel like you will die of old age before you finish. So, if you kind of hate planning and time management, this is probably why. But fear not— we will cover ways to make time less of a mystery.

O Say Can You See... Time Horizon

ADHD doesn't just impact how you see time in the moment. It also impacts how you see the future and what needs to be done when as future deadlines creep inexorably closer.

This brings us to a concept called *time horizon,* which is how close in time something needs to be for someone to consider acting on it. For example, if you have a big project due on Friday, when does it hit your mental radar and you start working on it? Monday? Thursday night? Saturday? Obviously, when you kick into gear depends on the situation—how important is the task? How fun or terrible will it be to do? What else do you have going on? In general, some people tend to activate on deadlines earlier while others tend to activate later. Again, I'll let you guess where folks with ADHD tend to cluster. I'll also let you guess what it means if you tend to ask *exactly* what time on Friday it's due.

When the task is boring and the consequences are further into the future, people with ADHD tend to have a shorter time horizon, meaning that tasks don't hit their mental radar until they get closer to the deadline. Before that, it's out there somewhere, in some sort of vague sense, but it's definitely not front and center in their thoughts. Perhaps there is some low level fretting about it, but they're not actively thinking about how to tackle the task or where it fits in the rest of their activities.

Russell Barkley, PhD says that ADHD causes future myopia. As in, people with ADHD don't see the future as clearly, just as people who need glasses don't see far away things as clearly. This leads to the (only somewhat) joking line that for people with ADHD there are two times: now and not now. Everything that isn't right now gets dumped into the not now bucket—tomorrow, next week, next year, the next millennium... Obviously, this is an over-simplification because people with ADHD can see the future, but there is definitely some truth to it at least in some moments. Whatever is happening right now looms large in the attention, but too often whatever is happening next is kind of like... whatever. And let's not even talk about what's happening after that—we'll get there when we get there. Presumably.

> You may be blind to time, but not to its consequences.

This occasional difficulty with seeing beyond now definitely impacts how people with ADHD manage their time and where they put their energy. This is why people with ADHD procrastinate—they don't look as far out into the future when they're considering what to work on next—until all of a sudden the future becomes the now and the deadline is upon them. Yikes!

This is why generic advice on time management and productivity falls flat for folks with ADHD (and frankly most people). To apply those strategies assumes that the person is thinking far enough into the future to activate themselves while they still have time for it. It sounds good and is easy to say, but is much harder to do, at least consistently. The only way to manage time better is to take this time blindness and shorter time horizon into account. Otherwise, it's just more obvious advice that you don't need more of—and failed strategies that you definitely don't need more of.

To counter this, time management strategies that are better targeted for folks with ADHD tend to fall into three general categories:

- **Supplement your internal sense of time** with plenty of clocks and external reminders. It's hard to do the right thing at the right time if you don't know what time it is. Counter time blindness by making time more visible. You can also make time more tangible by using analog clocks with hands that move, so that you can literally see the unstoppable march of time as the hand leaves one number behind and closes in on the next one.

- **Use alarms and other limits** (e.g., internet time limiters) to notify you that a specific time has arrived and that you should do something else. Make it easier to see that specific time rather than hoping that you will notice it on your own.

- **Use a schedule** to plan out your time, then check it occasionally so you know what you should be doing now. By assigning activities to future blocks of time, you're looking at the future and seeing yourself in it. You're thinking about the *not now*.

We will get into all sorts of variations, as well as what else gets in the way, in the rest of the book. Before you get there, read the next chapter, *3. ADHD Makes It Harder to Feel the Future*, where I talk about how ADHD affects motivation to work on those future tasks that you (hopefully) see.

Put It to Work

- Notice how difficulties with time awareness impact your ability to get stuff done—and stress. Are there certain activities where time slides by more invisibly? Or where you're better at noticing it?

- Notice how you think about future events and deadlines—when do you really start thinking about them in any kind of useful detail? How does this compare to when those around you start thinking about the same deadlines? How does that play out between you?

- What are some strategies that help you be more aware of time that you could use more often? How would they make your life easier?

• What, When, Where, and Why?

What strategies are you going to apply from this chapter? How will this be different from what you're already doing? Or perhaps have done before?

When and where? The more specific you can be, the better. Then actively look for these moments. Or set an alarm or other reminder to pull your attention to it. How can you set things up beforehand to make this easier to stick with?

Why? What problem will this solve or improve? What are all the direct and indirect benefits of this change? How is your life better for it? This is your motivation for when you don't feel like it.

3. ADHD Makes It Harder to Feel the Future

I N THE LAST CHAPTER, WE talked about how ADHD makes it harder to see time and future deadlines. That's the cognitive part. But what about the emotional and motivational part? As in, that feeling in your belly when you really, *really* don't want to do something? When it feels like moving a mountain to make yourself work on something? Yep, ADHD affects that, too. (Duh.)

The challenge for all of us is to sort through all the possible tasks that we could do in this moment and choose one. Some of those tasks are really fun but not necessarily that useful. Some are really important but painfully boring. And most tasks are somewhere in between. There's always more to do than time to do it, so we need to make choices—which means choosing one task and therefore not choosing all the rest. Until the next moment when we either choose to continue or to switch to something else.

All the while, we're being bombarded by stimuli from the world around us—pings from our phones, interrupting kids, the stack of laundry that's still sitting there, the banana we meant to eat an hour ago, that paperwork we need to fill out, etc. Look around you—how many things could you do just based on what is currently in your line of sight? Or open on your computer? Think about everything that comes at you in the morning routine. Or in a typical hour at work or school. It's a lot, right?

And then there are all those random thoughts—looking up that movie you heard about, making a dentist appointment, do we need milk?, that email that you're not sure what to do about, pressure to keep up with the social media onslaught, finding your partner to have some fun together, etc. And a bunch more etcs.

Our attention is constantly at work, deciding what to focus on—and what to screen out. Mostly screen out. Why is there always so much to screen out? As an example of your attention screening ability at work, what do your feet feel like? Now you know. Unless you were walking on cobblestones while reading this (possible but unlikely), you probably didn't care what your feet felt like, so your attention blocked it out from conscious awareness. And everything else except for the very limited number of stimuli that it let through. This process happens in every single moment as your attention scans the outer and inner world and decides what makes the cut. Sometimes it is best for your attention to stick to what it's on—as in, ignore the ping on your phone so you can click all the way through on submitting your taxes. At other times, it's best for your attention to shift—as in, look to see if it's that really important text you're waiting for.

In order to focus on what's most important (which usually means what is better for us in the future), we need to resist getting pulled onto all that other stuff vying for our attention, much of which is a lot more fun but probably not as beneficial. Of course, life can't be all work, so we also need to have fun and also sometimes to recharge by doing something kind of mindless. We need to keep it all in balance and decide, moment by moment, what is the best thing to do right now.

ADHD = Too Much Present, Not Enough Future

We all sometimes make choices that are more fun in the moment, even though we know that we will pay a price later. For example, watching one more episode and then feeling tired the next day. Ordering the fries instead of the salad and then feeling gross when we eat too many of them. Clicking over to social media "for just a quick sec" even though it never works out that way. People with ADHD just have these moments more often and maybe get stuck longer. They tend to be more pulled by whatever is more interesting in the moment, even if it's less helpful later. If you give them a hypothetical, they definitely know what the best thing to do is—people with ADHD have much more experience with negative consequences, so they *really* know. Unfortunately, with ADHD, there's a bigger bridge to cross between knowing and doing.

This is where *temporal discounting* comes in—the further into the future a consequence is, whether positive or negative, the less we feel it now and therefore the less weight we give it in our decision-making in the moment. We kind of put a thumb on the scale and do the thing in the moment that is a little worse for the future—not terrible, but not necessarily the best of the available options. For example, at 10:00 PM we really want the fun of watching another episode and don't care as much about feeling tired tomorrow. Of course, when tomorrow comes and we're paying the price, we will feel differently about that choice. In general, we all feel the temptations of the present more strongly than we feel the future negative cost and we feel the suffering of sacrifice in the moment more strongly than we feel the future benefits. We're not 100% objective about how we compare the present versus the future.

How strongly we feel a future consequence depends on a number of factors:

- **How far into the future is it?** The further into the future the consequence is, the less we feel it now—three months before the end of the semester, a missed assignment feels like no big deal but feels like a problem one week before.

- **How specific are the consequences?** Vague consequences are not motivating. For example, some sort of general decrease in health from vaping can feel rather unconvincing compared to what you know you gain from it in the moment.

- **How likely are the consequences?** We tend to be optimists about what we can get away with, especially if we really want to do something (or really don't). For example, if there's a chance that you won't get called out by your boss for being behind on your paperwork, you may decide to work on something less boring instead.

Temporal discounting explains why people make shortsighted choices on all sorts of things, such as smoking, not saving enough for retirement, procrastinating on important tasks, not putting things away which makes them harder to find later, etc. We sometimes fix the problems of the moment without thinking enough about how we're then creating possibly much bigger problems in the future.

> **By the time you feel it, it's too late.**
>
> *The slogan of ADHD time management*

People with ADHD *really* feel the present more than the future and are therefore less motivated to sacrifice the present for the future. It's an unfair fight where the present too often wins. This is why doing something fun (or at least less painful) right now feels better than making yourself work on that difficult project, even though you know you will be miserable staying up late tomorrow. The total suffering would be less if you worked on it earlier, but in the moment you can't connect to that future discomfort so you do something else instead. When tomorrow has become tonight and you're jammed up against the deadline (and the consequences!), *now* you feel the pressure to do it.

Temporal discounting explains why people with ADHD don't change their behavior from experience—again, it's not a problem of knowing, it's a problem of *doing*. As in, right now, in this moment, remembering and really feeling the misery of tomorrow night and deciding to bite the bullet and get half of the work done now so that tomorrow will be better. In order to feel the future consequences of our actions, we need to remember what similar past experiences felt like, then re-create that feeling now so we take the actions that will benefit us later. This is harder for folks with ADHD, so too often the feelings of the moment rule the day, and they pay the price tomorrow.

Of course, all of this presumes some sort of consideration and conscious choice, but sometimes the decision is made by circumstances. If you forget to do something, lose track of time, get distracted, or impulsively leap at something interesting, then there's no real choice being made. That option that would have benefitted your future never really had a chance. Granted, maybe some different choices earlier with more of an eye towards the future would have set up that situation differently, but in the moment, it isn't an intentional choice. Unfortunately, others may not believe that...

Feel the Future Now

Assuming our attention hasn't already been hijacked and we can make a conscious decision, we can try to compensate for temporal discounting. We can bring the future into the present by taking a moment to visualize how we will feel in the future if we do or don't act now—for example, prepping for that upcoming meeting versus doing something else instead. This needs to be a very intentional and effortful process to fight the automatic pull of temporal discounting and give the future a shot at winning over the temptations of the present.

- **Put yourself into that future moment** (e.g., sitting in that meeting). Picture yourself as vividly as possible—how will you feel? What will you think? What will you wish for? What will the scene look like? How would you describe it to someone else?

- **Compare and contrast acting and not acting now.** Put the scenarios side by side and really compare what they will each feel like.

- **How will future-you feel about present-you?** Will you look back on yesterday's you with appreciation or anger? What would you do if you were doing this for a friend? What would you tell future-you to explain the choice you made now?

The more you can bring the future into the present, the more likely you will be motivated into action. The more you can remind yourself that *you* will be the one paying the price or reaping the reward, not some vague future self, the easier it is to muster the motivation now. As my friend Stephanie Sarkis, PhD says, "What will my future-self thank me for doing now?" I would add that they might also curse you (but preferably not). It may sound weird to say, but we do kind of ignore the fact that *we* are the one who will suffer, as if we will somehow be able to pin it on someone else.

Definitely don't ask yourself if you want to do this now, because the answer is obviously no. You won't want to do it later either, but you won't have a choice, so that's the wrong question.

If you really want to be honest about what you're doing, then imagine having a conversation with your future self—as in, the you who, in that future moment, is paying the price for your procrastinating now. For example, the one who is staying up late tomorrow night to finish what you're trying to wiggle out of doing now. What would tomorrow-night-you say to now-you? They're pretty mad, right? And what would you say to defend your decision to watch cat videos rather than start that project? Pretty weak, right? Do you think tomorrow-night-you is buying any of it? They're not, because they know you make crap up when you don't want to do something. For more on our sometimes impressive ability to convince ourselves of bad ideas, check out *23. The Lies We Tell Ourselves*.

If only someone could invent an app that allows future-us to call and yell at now-us before we do anything that screws them, the world would be a very different place. Kale would be king.

Artificial Consequences are Better than Natural Ones

A lot of managing ADHD is about setting things up beforehand and creating a good environment, rather than trying to not be distracted by distractions and tempted by temptations. I'm all in favor of believing in yourself, but...

We're all more likely to be happy with what we did if we bring the future into the present by creating some more motivating consequences for ourselves. We can set up the types of consequences that will nudge us towards better choices in those difficult moments, rather than being limited to what we know might possibly happen (a.k.a., natural consequences). The problem with natural consequences is that they can take too long to show up—the cost of not hanging up your towel isn't paid until tomorrow when it's cold and wet. Or they may not show up at all—you don't get called on in class so you get away with not doing the reading. Or they are

> To be more productive, give the future a fighting chance over the present.

initially paid by someone else—your spouse is the one annoyed that you didn't clean up the kitchen. In these ways and others, there's often too loose a connection between actions and consequences, which can make it easy to talk ourselves into questionable actions, especially if you have ADHD.

If you want to make it more likely that you will do that better thing that your future self will thank you for, then you can tilt the odds in a number of ways. It's your life—take charge of it by making consequences more:

- **Immediate**—e.g., you can get a snack when you complete the expense report

- **Frequent**—e.g., more progress check-ins with your boss to keep you on track

- **External**—e.g., tell a coworker you have to buy them lunch if you're late for the meeting so there is a tangible consequence

- **Salient/important**—e.g., tell your romantic partner you will do the dishes if you don't text to say you will be late (so forgetting bothers you more)

- **Consistent**—e.g., you can't leave work until you enter the day's customer contacts into the database, no matter what

There are a million variations on these five ideas, so customize them to the situation whenever you can. Identify the situations that give you the most trouble and figure out your best options. The more tricks you have up your sleeve, the more productive you will be.

Put It to Work

- Notice how your feelings about a future event or deadline change as time passes. Is it gradual or more sudden? When does it cross the threshold into action?

- Practice feeling the future in order to change what you do in the moment. Pick some upcoming deadlines and imagine yourself in that future moment. How will you feel if you start working earlier versus later? How does putting yourself into that future moment affect your motivation now?

- Identify places where you can bring the future into the present by adjusting the artificial consequences. What are the most effective ways to incentivize yourself, especially on the tasks that you have the most trouble getting to?

• What, When, Where, and Why?

What strategies are you going to apply from this chapter? How will this be different from what you're already doing? Or perhaps have done before?

When and where? The more specific you can be, the better. Then actively look for these moments. Or set an alarm or other reminder to pull your attention to it. How can you set things up beforehand to make this easier to stick with?

Why? What problem will this solve or improve? What are all the direct and indirect benefits of this change? How is your life better for it? This is your motivation for when you don't feel like it.

4. Co-Occurring Conditions Make Everything Harder

ADHD USUALLY DOESN'T TRAVEL ALONE, especially when it's undiagnosed and untreated. Anxiety, depression, substance overuse, sleep problems, and general burnout are all more likely if you're not managing your ADHD well. Then there are all the impacts on your physical health—like if you keep forgetting to do your PT exercises so your back keeps hurting when you sit at your desk too long.

Obviously, the more struggles you have, the harder everything is going to be, including your ability to get things done. ADHD makes it hard enough to focus without anxious thoughts filling your attention. ADHD procrastination doesn't get any better when the weight of depression makes it even harder to get going.

Also, multiple conditions can get tangled together and each can make it harder to address the others—for example, being sleep deprived makes it harder to sustain attention on boring tasks, and having ADHD makes it harder to manage time so you can get to bed when you should. Stuck.

When an adult contacts me for an ADHD evaluation, they've often been treated for something else first, usually anxiety or depression. Kids and teens who haven't suffered as much yet may just have ADHD. Unfortunately, the adults have suffered. They have plenty of ADHD-related reasons to be anxious and depressed, beyond all the other reasons that anyone might have. Therefore, whatever other treatment they've had was probably somewhat helpful, but never quite accomplished everything they hoped for. This is because other treatments, especially medication, for other conditions don't do much for ADHD. And working on anxiety or depression in the face of continuing ADHD setbacks is like painting the water stains on the ceiling but not fixing the roof first—it only looks good until the next rain. Similarly, untreated ADHD will keep serving up new reasons to feel anxious and depressed. Getting treated for one's ADHD is that crucial missing piece.

> If you have (untreated) ADHD and you're not at least a little anxious or depressed, then you're not paying attention...

For this reason, I always hope that treating a client's ADHD will have some spillover benefit on other conditions. This is reasonable when a lot of what is driving those other conditions is related to the fallout of untreated ADHD. You get a two-for-one, both with feeling worse and also with feeling better. Getting on top of your ADHD (enough) so you can live a better life and feel better about yourself tends to have the added benefit of improving all those other conditions. It also tends to make it easier to be consistent with the interventions targeting those other conditions, like exercising more for anxiety or being more social for depression. And if medication is being considered, you can usually get ADHD meds dialed in more quickly than other medications. The exception might be when another condition is more significantly impacting someone's life functioning—as in, they're so depressed that not much is going to happen until that's knocked down a few notches.

Having said that, there are plenty of non-ADHD reasons to feel anxious or depressed, drink too much, have trouble sleeping, etc., so sometimes that other condition needs to be treated more directly, rather than hoping for that two-for-one from addressing the ADHD. If something other than ADHD is eroding your happiness, then take it seriously and do what you need to do to feel and function better. If you're unable to get to a better place with it on your own or by talking to family and friends, then it may be time to consider some professional intervention. You can start with your primary care clinician who may be able to recommend a therapist and perhaps handle medication, if needed. You can also ask the people you know, including any other treatment providers, for recommendations. Look folks up online, find out about the financials (fees, insurance reimbursement, etc.), and see if you can have a brief call to feel them out. It can take some persistence to find the right fit, but it's worth the investment. And if the person you're seeing isn't quite right, then find someone better.

Addressing these other conditions isn't just about productivity; it's about feeling good in your life, feeling good about yourself. It can be easy to lose sight of this or to over-focus on your struggles more than your successes, especially when seen through the lens of anxiety and depression. So put in the effort, give yourself credit for that effort, and make a point of noticing the results.

Put It to Work

- Reflect on whether some other condition is making your life harder than it needs to be. What are all the ways that it affects how you feel and function?

- How do your ADHD struggles contribute to another condition? Remember this as (yet another) motivation to work on your ADHD. Or is the other condition mostly unrelated to your ADHD?

- If another condition is casting too dark a shadow on your happiness, reach out to at least one family member, friend, or professional to talk about it. If necessary, research clinicians you could see.

- ## What, When, Where, and Why?

What strategies are you going to apply from this chapter? How will this be different from what you're already doing? Or perhaps have done before?

When and where? The more specific you can be, the better. Then actively look for these moments. Or set an alarm or other reminder to pull your attention to it. How can you set things up beforehand to make this easier to stick with?

Why? What problem will this solve or improve? What are all the direct and indirect benefits of this change? How is your life better for it? This is your motivation for when you don't feel like it.

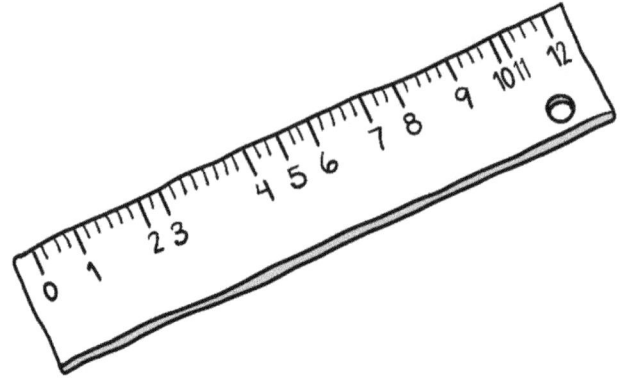

5. Why Am I So Maddeningly Inconsistent?

RUSSELL BARKLEY, PHD HAS A famous quote that ADHD is not a disorder of knowing what to do; it's a disorder of doing what you know. I use that line all the time. I even used that same sentence to start Chapter 1. If anything, folks with ADHD know far better what they should do because they've been told far more often what to do. Knowledge is not the problem here, folks.

Interestingly (and confusingly and maddeningly), sometimes doing isn't entirely the problem either. As in, doing something once is easy—it's doing it every time and at the right time that's hard. Let's throw in doing it at the right place for bonus points. It's the predictability and consistency that's the problem. People who don't have ADHD just have an easier time kind of plowing through and getting things done, regardless of how they feel or how boring the task is. But if you have ADHD, your performance is much more influenced by how interesting the task

> Knowledge may be power, but ADHD pulls the plug.

is, competing options, social pressure, energy level, novelty... and total randomness. All of this makes it feel like it's hard to plan—or pointless.

The times that you do get things done can sometimes feel like a double-edged sword because they prove that you *can* do it—which then kind of makes it look like a choice when you can't get it in gear. Here we go again... It's easy to beat yourself up about it, and unfortunately some people will be happy to take a few shots, too (which is why I have an entire section on this: *VII. The Social Side of Productivity*).

But all is not lost! ADHD is at its worst when you don't know that that's what's getting in the way or when you haven't yet figured out how to work with it. In this case, knowledge is indeed power if it explains your struggles more accurately and suggests better strategies. The whole point of managing your ADHD is not only to be more productive in total, but also to be more consistent and predictable. Less randomness. Less dependent on the crushing pressure of a looming deadline. This makes life much less stressful and gives you more time and energy for the other good things because you're spending less

> ADHD is all about *performance.* Therefore, solutions are all about the *point of performance.*

time grinding away or fretting about not yet grinding away. That's the reward for the hard work of managing your ADHD better, for committing yourself to the strategies in this book.

Accept that Variability

You'll never be as consistent as a Swiss watch (no one is, except for Swiss watchmakers); there will still be those times when things just don't click. Fine, good enough. It's a lot easier to cut yourself some slack if you feel like you're generally putting in the effort, that you tried, but this just isn't going to be one of those times when it works out. By having a bit of compassion for yourself, you're less likely to spiral and burn even more time beating yourself up so you get even less done. If you find yourself spinning out, take a breather and maybe walk away if you can. Some push-ups or squats may burn off some of that agitation. Remind yourself that this one moment doesn't define you and that there are plenty of times when you are able to get things done. Accept that this task isn't getting done right now, but maybe there is something else that you might be able to chip away at. Or maybe you need to do something mindless for a little bit. Once you feel settled again, reflect on what happened that knocked your progress out of gear on this task. Anything to learn here?

The social bonus for handling these situations with more grace is that it's more likely that others will also be more understanding and even helpful. They may still be disappointed that you didn't get that task done, but may feel that you're more approachable about it so there's hope it will get addressed next time.

You may also want to think about what to say in these situations so the other person isn't left to infer what is going on with you and what to expect next. It's useful to have some prepared wording that you know well and can say easily. It's likely to come out much better than winging it when you're feeling frustrated. You might say something like, "Sometimes I just get stuck in neutral and can't get going, no matter how hard I try. It's usually better if I do something else first and come back around to it." Say it with some empathy for the impact on the other person, but also state it kind of matter-of-factly, so it doesn't come across as negotiable. We'll get into all of this more in *VII. The Social Side of Productivity*, but if your dealings with others are causing you undue stress and grief, feel free to skip ahead.

Put It to Work

- Look for some moments where a little self-compassion would serve you well. What can you tell yourself? Then notice how that compassion gets you back on track more quickly than beating yourself up.

- When you catch yourself having an ADHD moment, take a couple deep breaths, then do the next good thing when you can. Or some other good thing.

- Craft some wording to explain ADHD variability to yourself—and to others. Then practice saying it out loud so you can say it calmly and confidently when you need it.

- ## What, When, Where, and Why?

What strategies are you going to apply from this chapter? How will this be different from what you're already doing? Or perhaps have done before?

When and where? The more specific you can be, the better. Then actively look for these moments. Or set an alarm or other reminder to pull your attention to it. How can you set things up beforehand to make this easier to stick with?

Why? What problem will this solve or improve? What are all the direct and indirect benefits of this change? How is your life better for it? This is your motivation for when you don't feel like it.

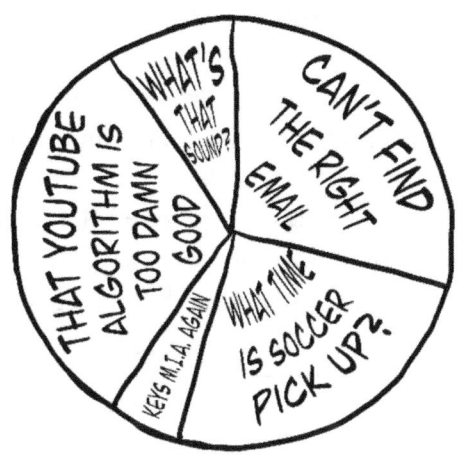

6. What Exactly Is Getting in Your Way Here?

WHEN A CLIENT COMPLAINS ABOUT being stuck or unable to get something done, we start by understanding the situation (like, really understanding) and identifying exactly what's getting in their way. Sometimes it's obvious (not usually), but most of the time it's more complicated than it initially seemed, or there were other facets of the situation that were tripping them up. It's tempting to jump straight into solutions, but you want the *right* solutions, which means first being really clear on the problem. This is as true of productivity as it is of medical treatments or tech support. This is also why you're currently holding a book and not a pamphlet. People are complicated; there are lots of moving parts, so we have lots of ways of getting tripped up.

Let's start by crossing some potential problems off the list. If the problem is ADHD, then the problem isn't character, laziness, intelligence, irresponsibility... or anything else you've been accused of. Or

> A problem well defined is a problem half solved.

beaten yourself up with. It's not to say that those aren't also potential problems, but if it's really your ADHD that's the culprit, then you don't need to add in those other problems to explain why you're stuck. Unfortunately, ADHD can kind of look like these other problems, so it's easy to jump to conclusions. Besides the fact that these other problems make you feel terrible about yourself, identifying the wrong problem tends to suggest unhelpful solutions, so you stay stuck. This is the power of an accurate diagnosis—it points you towards solutions that are much more likely to actually work and then keep working.

> "Alarms don't work for me because I just turn them off and then don't do it."
> Or to do list, schedule, fancy app, whiteboard...

It's an obvious suggestion to use alarms to remind you that a certain time has arrived. It offloads memory and tracking time to a tool that frankly does a much better job of it than our brains do. Even so, I've had clients reject the idea because they just turn the alarm off and keep doing what they were doing. Based on this, it's easy to conclude that alarms don't work. Actually, the alarm worked perfectly—it notified the person that a particular time had arrived. That's it. Mission accomplished. What alarms *don't* do is motivate you to do the task— they don't make threats or give you a cookie. On the plus side, if you know that's it's now time to leave for that meeting, you now have a shot at getting there on time, more than you did if the time quietly slid by.

What this comes down to is the difference between necessary and sufficient— knowing the time is helpful but by itself doesn't get the job done. This is why so many strategies you've tried didn't live up to your hopes and dreams—they might have been necessary, but they weren't sufficient. Just today, I had a client show up late despite being very proud of herself for setting a bunch of alarms beforehand—unfortunately, she didn't first gather up all the stuff she needed, so she still had to run around and find everything. So close!

The same problem of necessary but not sufficient goes for all that well-meaning (but often unrequested) advice you've gotten when someone says that "you just need to do..." First of all, you've probably already tried it, but thanks anyway. Second, any time someone says "just," we should all be skeptical. Maybe more so if you have ADHD because it's probably ignoring some of the other necessary factors.

Except for the simple stuff, like shooting off a quick reply to a text, in order to do the right things at the right times, we need to hit the mark in three broad ways:

- **Planning**: knowing *what* needs to be done *when*

- **Awareness**: knowing what needs to be done *in this moment*

- **Motivation**: feeling the *drive* to actually do what we know

All three are necessary; none are sufficient. There are a whole bunch of ways that things can break down in each of these three areas, which is why it can feel so difficult to march from start to finish. Again, this is why you're holding a book and not a pamphlet. The goal of every other page here is to help you identify what's getting in your way and give you some more targeted solutions.

As some examples, where are things breaking down?

- **Planning**:
  o Forgetting to put the task into your schedule or to do list
  o Feeling anxious about the task and "forgetting" to put it into your schedule or to do list
  o Not setting an alarm
  o Starting an engrossing activity right before the task you're supposed to do
  o Procrastinating on earlier tasks so you now have to focus on them instead
  o Forgetting an earlier commitment that then becomes the top priority

- **Awareness**:
  o Not realizing what time it is or what should happen now
  o Being hyperfocused on another task and not realizing you need to switch gears

- o Turning off an alarm, but then returning to the original task "for just a minute" and getting hyperfocused again

- o Forgetting important aspects or requirements of the task and then missing the mark

- o Impulsively jumping to another task first (to "get it out of the way")

- **Motivation**:

  - o Not actually caring about the task and therefore choosing to not do it

  - o The task feels too much like someone else's agenda

  - o Just plain tired

  - o Something else (anything else) is much more interesting

  - o Avoiding it because it's not clear what you're supposed to do, you feel overwhelmed, or you're worried that it won't go well

  - o The deadline feels too far away to feel motivating now

Separating out these three domains is helpful because it puts your energy where it's most effective. As we all know, a beeping alarm that resulted from good planning and created increased awareness isn't helpful if your motivation is MIA in that moment. As you read the rest of the book, you will come across a lot of reasons why people struggle with productivity. My goal is not to show you that you have more problems than you previously thought, but rather to empower you to actively address what's getting in your way by getting really clear about the problem so you can match the best solutions.

Put It to Work

- Think about some recent situations that didn't work out well. What exactly made a better outcome less likely? Did it break down in planning, awareness, or motivation?

- Think about some recent situations that did work out well. What exactly made a better outcome more likely? What did you do to strengthen planning, awareness, and motivation?

- Where do things tend to break down for you in planning, awareness, and motivation? What can you do to overcome these sticking points? This is your shortlist to keep an eye out for.

- ## What, When, Where, and Why?

  What strategies are you going to apply from this chapter? How will this be different from what you're already doing? Or perhaps have done before?

  When and where? The more specific you can be, the better. Then actively look for these moments. Or set an alarm or other reminder to pull your attention to it. How can you set things up beforehand to make this easier to stick with?

  Why? What problem will this solve or improve? What are all the direct and indirect benefits of this change? How is your life better for it? This is your motivation for when you don't feel like it.

SECTION II. SET A BETTER FOUNDATION

A BIG PART OF MANAGING ADHD involves making the most of what you've got—same as for everyone else, but maybe extra important if you really want to perform well. This means bringing as much of your A game as possible. Maybe your B game. Definitely not your "Incomplete—Did not turn in final" game. Unfortunately, motivating for boring jobs and paying attention to all the details is hard enough without dragging yourself through sleep-deprivation fog or feeling like a hangry monster. I won't suggest that you need to live like a monk, but this is where improved productivity begins, so the investment will pay off. As my friend Alan Brown (the ADD Crusher) says, time management really begins with energy management and you want to start out with a full battery. A lot of stuff in this section might feel like yet another boring obligation that you don't have time for but are supposed to do anyway, but it does pay off, I promise.

Of course, the double whammy of ADHD is that it makes it harder to be consistent about the things that will bring your best performance. Therefore, we're going to aspire to greatness, but with a fat helping of compassion for when things don't work out—and with a healthy dose of persistence to get back on the horse. Your brain cells do their best work when you get enough sleep, exercise regularly, and eat a generally healthy diet, so these are a good place to put some energy—and to remind yourself that doing even a little better is still worth it.

All of this boring but important consistency tends to be easier to pull off if you're taking medication, so we'll talk about how to think about that decision. Some people swear by meds, whereas others swear at the thought of them. We live in politically polarized times, but the ADHD community was into strong opposing positions before it was cool. This chapter won't tell you what to do (or shame you for your position), but it will help you think through the psychologically loaded question of taking a medication that (kind of) changes your thinking, at least temporarily.

Our brains are important, but we're more than just squishy, mobile bags of electrolytes. All this work you're putting in to change your productivity habits takes a lot of energy, so it needs to feel worthwhile, like there's enough of a payoff. The less obvious part of habit change is to notice the changes that you're making, especially if they are more incremental than orgasmic. Progress is important, but so are appropriate expectations.

And finally, you're not doing this alone. The question is whether the people in your life are a wind at your back or complaints behind your back. We all benefit from a cheering section, especially when we're trying to do something that doesn't come easily.

A good foundation makes your desired outcomes more likely and more in your control, with less dependence on luck, so let's set you up to kick some ass.

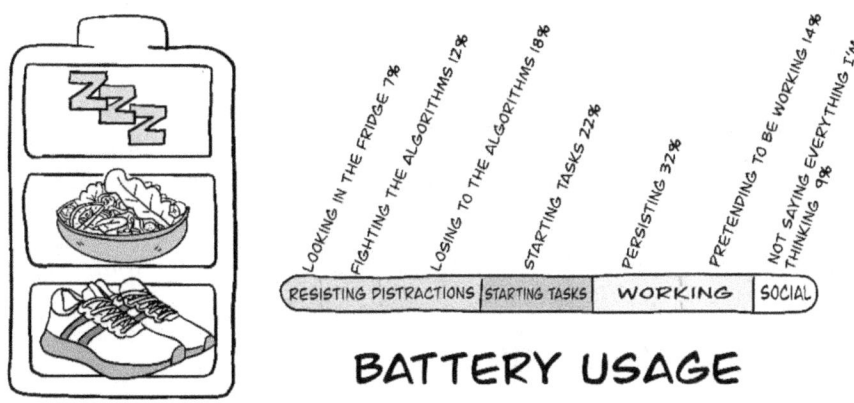

LOOKING IN THE FRIDGE 7%
FIGHTING THE ALGORITHMS 12%
LOSING TO THE ALGORITHMS 18%
STARTING TASKS 22%
PERSISTING 32%
PRETENDING TO BE WORKING 14%
NOT SAYING EVERYTHING I'M THINKING 9%

| RESISTING DISTRACTIONS | STARTING TASKS | WORKING | SOCIAL |

BATTERY USAGE

7. Make the Most of Your Brain: Sleep, Diet & Exercise

I OFTEN ASK CLIENTS ABOUT their sleep, diet, and exercise because it can make such a difference in how they feel and function. And because ADHD makes all of it harder. The good news is that you don't need to be a vegan triathlete to feel and function better. Even partial improvements like going to bed half an hour earlier will make a noticeable difference, especially as you start racking up more days that are a little better.

What makes these better habits hard to maintain is that they take work or sacrifice in the moment so you can (generally speaking) feel better later. As we talked about in *2. ADHD Makes It Harder to See Time* and *3. ADHD Makes It Harder to Feel the Future*, these are not the situations where folks with ADHD tend to shine. Even so, it's worth the effort to try to do a bit better here, especially if you're more at the long-

> By the time you feel it, it's too late.
> —The problem with bad habits.

haul-trucker-on-meth end of the self-care spectrum. Or have the sleep habits of a vampire (The sun! It burns!).

There's a lot more to be said about sleep, diet, and exercise than this little ol' chapter, but if you're frustrated with your level of productivity, this might be a likely culprit and therefore worth the effort. Also, by the way, feeling better and getting more done today or tomorrow is a way more convincing argument for healthy habits than some possible negative outcome twenty years from now.

ADHD Makes Sleep Harder

Before we talk about how to be nicer to your neurons, let's list some of the ways that the cards are stacked against you when it comes to sleep:

- ADHD folks tend to be night owls
- Earlier procrastination requires later activity that can delay getting into bed
- Meds may interfere with sleep (and may also help you get things done earlier so you can actually hit your bedtime)
- It's easier to focus when everything is quiet at night
- You finally get me-time at night after a busy day (revenge bedtime procrastination)
- You lose track of time and unintentionally stay up too late (but also sometimes that unintentional is kind of intentional)
- Chronic sleep deprivation feels normal so this is just life, right?

As always, getting more sleep is easier said than done—sometimes *much* easier— but it's worth the effort. Here are a number of strategies:

- Make a real commitment to value sleep—and really remind yourself of the benefits
- Create (and honor!) a bedtime and maybe even set an alarm for when to call it a day and get into bed

- Avoid jet lagging yourself by sleeping late on weekends because it will set your clock later for Monday (and probably Tuesday)
- Avoid napping more than twenty minutes and also any napping in the last third of the day because it will dysregulate your nighttime sleep
- Be more productive during the day so you can clock out earlier (every little bit helps)
- Do your nighttime routine right after taking care of the kids or dog, even if you stay up after, so you're a few steps closer
- Get into bed together with your partner (and don't believe yourself that you'll be up in five minutes)
- Use a habit tracker app, then get kind of annoying by talking about it all the time
- Make a bet with your romantic partner about how long you can keep the streak alive
- Listen to relaxation, mindfulness, or soundscape audio to quiet the mind once in bed
- Don't over-rely on melatonin to undo your other sleep sins

Exercise Benefits Your Brain

There are the obvious (and boring) physical health reasons to exercise regularly, but I think the much more convincing argument is that exercise creates an immediate benefit to attention, memory, complex problem-solving, and mood. Your brain works better after you exercise. That's way more motivating than some far off and far from guaranteed benefit to your weight or blood pressure or something. The best way to get someone with ADHD to not do something is to make the consequences far off and far from guaranteed.

When it comes to exercise, anything is better than nothing. Sort of. Taking a walk around the block is better than another uninterrupted hour at your desk, but the real benefits of exercise require real effort. You need to be sweating and for more than a few minutes. Other than that, it doesn't matter what you do, as long as you keep showing up. If you get bored easily, then mix it up. Definitely make it enjoyable or at least enjoyable enough. If it's boring, inconvenient, annoying, frustrating, or you just kind of hate it, then you definitely won't continue with it. That's not even an ADHD thing—that's human nature.

Sometimes the hardest part is the first five minutes, so just focus on getting started. If you can get yourself moving, you'll probably keep moving. If you start exercising and just aren't feeling it, fine. Try again tomorrow. If you're more likely to show up and to get a better workout when you do it with someone else, then find a buddy or do a class. Or pair working out with some guilty pleasure such as watching that trashy series that you secretly love or listening to songs with tons of inappropriate content that get you too many questions from your kids and too many eyerolls from your spouse.

When you do get a workout in, make a point of noticing how the hours after working out are more productive, how you have more energy, how your mood is a bit brighter, how you're less stressed and maybe even sleep a little better. This is your sales pitch to yourself the next time you're tempted to bail because you're just not feeling it. This is how to convince yourself that it's worth the initial blah. Hell, record a motivational video after you worked out and are all fired up.

Brain Fuel

Dietary changes or supplements won't treat ADHD, but we all do better with a generally healthy diet and without going too long between eating. Unfortunately, healthy eating often takes at least some planning ahead and good time management in multiple moments. This can be the first to go when you're feeling overwhelmed. Yet another easier said than done. There's also the issue that waiting too long to eat because you're hyperfocused or don't have time is a set-up to then wolf down whatever you can get your hands on, which is probably not a healthy salad.

So let's keep it simple. Stay away from the quick fixes, expensive supplements, and complications with big promises and marginal benefits—life's hard enough. A healthy diet follows the basics, which is easier to pull off anyway. Keep the unhealthy temptations as far away as possible—as in, leave them at the store rather than in the cabinet where it takes *way* more willpower to not grab. If a family member wants that stuff around, see if you can find options that you don't like as much. Find easy, generally healthy foods you can snack on to keep your blood sugar steady, especially if your meds make you less interested in big lunches. Being hangry makes you not only less productive, but also a lot less fun to hang out with.

Process > Outcome

When it comes to habit change, focus on creating and living a good process. Or good enough. As in, the habits that will generally help you feel better and set a good foundation for a more productive day such as getting into bed around ten. Bigger outcomes, like losing weight, can take too long to show meaningful progress let alone finish, so it's easy to get discouraged if you need that big payoff. Instead, make the goal to keep doing this better habit rather than reaching the final outcome—working out three times a week rather than losing ten pounds.

Then, find ways to slide into doing it rather than slide away from it. Get momentum on your side. Relying on willpower to muscle through something annoying sounds great for, like, five minutes but has a pretty short shelf life. The better approach is to find ways to streamline the process so it takes less forcing yourself to do it—that willpower muscle tires out pretty quickly. For example, bringing your gym bag and a snack with you to work so you can hit the gym right after—home has way too much gravitational pull and you're less likely to break free if you swing by to change.

> Partial progress is still progress! Make today a good day regardless of what happened yesterday.

Then take pride in every time you act on this good habit. Notice and give yourself credit for each small action you take. Remind yourself of the benefits and why you're doing it. This means not just the negatives you will avoid (like being tired tomorrow) but the positives you will gain (better mood at work and maybe you can leave early to do something fun). Those positives are way more motivating, so focus on those. Too much of living with ADHD can feel like trying to avoid negatives, which is a low bar for a satisfying life. When you do have setbacks, handle them resiliently, without catastrophizing, and get back on the horse. What's the next good thing you can do?

59

Put It to Work

- What is at least one thing you can do to get a better night's sleep? How much better would you feel and function if you were well rested?

- Identify one way to add more exercise to your day and a few ways to add more exercise to your week. How much better would you feel and function if you moved more?

- Identify one way to improve your eating habits today and a few ways to improve them this week. How much better would you feel and function if you ate better?

- ## What, When, Where, and Why?

What strategies are you going to apply from this chapter? How will this be different from what you're already doing? Or perhaps have done before?

When and where? The more specific you can be, the better. Then actively look for these moments. Or set an alarm or other reminder to pull your attention to it. How can you set things up beforehand to make this easier to stick with?

Why? What problem will this solve or improve? What are all the direct and indirect benefits of this change? How is your life better for it? This is your motivation for when you don't feel like it.

8. Should You Take Medication?

STIMULANT MEDICATION FOR ADHD continues to be more controversial than it should be, given what the science says. The research is really clear that stimulants tend to work quite well, the risks are low, and the side effects can usually be managed. If you look at the group averages, there's a lot to like about the stimulants. The odds are in your favor that they will be helpful, but you as one person are not a group average, so the only way to know what they can do for you is to try them.

There are certainly people with ADHD who do well without medication, but most folks will probably have to work a lot harder without it. There's also the question of what level of performance you're looking for. And how many ADHD moments you're willing to tolerate. As a simple example, I often don't put my contact lenses in on Sundays, and it works out just fine as long as I'm not driving anywhere. The rest of the week though, my life is more fulfilling by being

> Strategies only work when you use them. (And alternatives aren't treatments.)

able to drive at night. I could live without contacts if I had to, but it would be smaller and more restricted than I would want.

There are a number of ways to describe what medication does:

- It helps people with ADHD do what they know

- It closes the gap between intentions and actions

- It helps the executive functions operate more reliably

- It gives your brain an extra moment of pause before reacting

- It makes it easier to resist distractions and temptations

- It makes you more consistent and predictable

- It gives you better emotional regulation

None of this is magic. Medication doesn't do the work for you, and it doesn't make boring tasks exciting. But, overall, it tends to have a positive effect on productivity—not just at work, but also at home and with personal matters such as relationships and self-care. Ultimately, it gives you more mental bandwidth to pursue what is really important in your life. So although there are risks and side effects to every treatment, there are also risks and side effects to not using this treatment. You need to make your own decision about whether this is something that would be helpful at this point in your life. My only hope is that it's based on accurate information from reputable sources combined with a clear understanding of your situation and options.

Let's start with the elephant in the room: for the vast majority of folks with ADHD, the stimulants are not addictive. If you take too much, you will probably feel worse and tell your prescriber to lower the dose. If anything, it's untreated ADHD that is the risk factor for substance abuse and addiction—and stimulant medication potentially provides some protective effect. Also, research shows that adults with ADHD who are trying to stay sober from alcohol and other drugs are more

> If stimulants are so addictive, then why do so many of my clients forget to take them?

likely to retain their sobriety when they're treated with a stimulant. That totally makes sense.

Get It Right

If you are going to try medication then do it right so you really know what it can do for you. Most people find the extended-release stimulants to be the most effective by far and way more effective than the non-stimulants. The most commonly used extended-release stimulants are names that you probably already know: Adderall XR, Concerta, and Vyvanse, all of which are available in generic. Unlike the short-acting versions of the same medications, they hopefully last all day with fewer peaks and valleys. Also, needing to take pills in the middle of the day is a great way to forget to take pills in the middle of the day. If you find that even the extended-release versions peter out too early, you can add in a short-acting booster dose around dinner (for when the maid and butler have the night off).

When I have clients who are working with a prescriber to figure out their medication regimen, I say that I'm impatient and greedy. I want them to get to an effective dose quickly, and I want them to get the greatest benefit from it that they can. There's no need to waste a few months at partially effective doses before finally getting it right. And, by analogy, when I go to the eye doctor, I want to be able to see all seven rows in the vision chart, not just the top two.

The standard protocol is that you start on a low dose, which probably doesn't do much of anything. You can then increase it about once a week (not once a month as with the antidepressants) until you get to an effective dose. The only thing you're treating by taking so long to get to the right dose is youth.

> If you can't tell whether or not your medication is working, then it's not working.

I make a point of asking clients what they notice from their medication and look for three things:

- **Can you definitely tell the difference?** I'm looking for a definitive answer about what the medication is doing for them—and that the people who know them well clearly see an improvement. Unclear or unimpressive benefits suggest that the dose is too low.

- **Does it last 10-12 hours?** It's sometimes easier to know how long it lasts than to judge how well it's working (compared to what?), so this can help you dial in the right dose. If it's not lasting long enough, the dose may be too low. Related to this, when someone can't tell when it wears off, it's probably because it isn't doing much when it's on. Fortunately, both duration and effectiveness will improve at the right dose.

- **Is it still equally effective after a week?** Sometimes a low dose will work really well for a day or two then drop off. If so, you're probably close to the right dose but need to go up a little bit.

Just as we tell a kid staring skeptically at a vegetable to try it before making any judgments, the way to make the most fully informed decision about medication is to try it and see what difference it makes for you. If you aren't that impressed, then you may want to talk to your prescriber to see if anything can be done to improve it—or find a new prescriber for a second opinion.

If you haven't yet tried medication but are struggling more than you want to be, including in applying all these awesome strategies that you keep meaning to use, then you may want to consider giving it a try. Keep in mind that it's not that momentous a decision—it's not like getting a face tattoo. If you don't find it helpful or decide that you don't need it, then you just don't take it again tomorrow. Done. I've certainly had clients who decide to stop their medication, but I've also had plenty of folks who lament not having tried it sooner. It's really about taking the time to make a good choice for your life right now.

Alternatives Aren't Treatments

ADHD seems to have more than its fair share of ineffective treatments that carry big claims but no research. Let's start with what actually does have research support. Medication has thousands of solid research studies showing its safety and effectiveness. Therapy, coaching and mindfulness have been shown to help with certain aspects of living with ADHD and managing some of the symptoms or at least reducing their negative impact on people's lives.

That's it. Nothing else works: dietary changes, nutritional supplements, chiropractic interventions, brain balance exercises, natural remedies, brain training programs, etc. Not only has research shown these to be ineffective, but in some cases, we would need to completely re-write our understanding of neurology and ADHD in order for these to possibly work.

You can obviously try anything you want, but I would make the case that there is a cost in trying interventions that are unlikely to be helpful. Besides the time, effort, and financial expense, there is also a cost in dashed optimism—no one needs another dead end. Plus, time spent on ineffective interventions delays more effective interventions which means more preventable suffering.

Put It to Work

- Make an effort to notice the variety of ways that ADHD impacts your productivity this week.

- If you take medication for ADHD, is it as effective as it should be and at the right times? If not, talk to your prescriber. Same for if the side effects are worse than you wish them to be.

- If you don't take medication for ADHD, get clear on why you don't. Does this decision still work for you? How do you feel about your current level of performance? What does it take to get there?

- **What, When, Where, and Why?**

What strategies are you going to apply from this chapter? How will this be different from what you're already doing? Or perhaps have done before?

When and where? The more specific you can be, the better. Then actively look for these moments. Or set an alarm or other reminder to pull your attention to it. How can you set things up beforehand to make this easier to stick with?

Why? What problem will this solve or improve? What are all the direct and indirect benefits of this change? How is your life better for it? This is your motivation for when you don't feel like it.

9. Give Yourself Some Credit: Notice Your Successes

UNFORTUNATELY, OUR BAD EXPERIENCES are easier to notice—and remember—than the good ones. The negatives tend to grab awareness and stick in memory better than the positives. It feels terrible, but there is a protective effect to remembering what to avoid next time—hopefully while there's still time to do something different rather than after. (Damnit! Again!) Unfortunately, ADHD can give you not only more frequent negative experiences, but also experiences that are more visible to others. Even if things end well, you may know everything that went on behind the scenes and therefore write off the success. As the saying (sort of) goes, you may snatch defeat from the jaws of victory.

This negative filter can also impact both what you notice and what you give more weight to when you work on learning new habits—like when you're working through this book. You might need to put a thumb on the scale to counterbalance that negative bias.

To do this, actively look for and give yourself credit for the effort that you are putting in:

- On the good habits you were already doing

- Every time you pick up this book and reflect on how to apply a new idea to your life

- On the new strategies that you try out

- When you have a setback and get yourself back on track

Good effort doesn't guarantee success, but it makes it more likely and it's the part that we can have the most influence on. Learning good lessons and then applying them forward is the second key to success.

What Should Progress Look Like?

What is reasonable to expect for a new habit? Everything seems easy until we actually need to do it, especially if it's something that we need to do tomorrow or next week. We're all happy to commit our future selves to all sorts of drudgery and challenges. Alternatively, we may feel like we've seen this movie before and don't have a lot of faith that this new habit will stick.

How satisfied you are with your progress will depend not only on what you do, but also on how it matches up to your expectations. I'm all in favor of pushing yourself to greatness, but if you set the bar too high, perhaps to counteract all those definitely not great times, then you're more likely to notice the ways that you fall short. When it comes to habit change, persistence is far more important than perfection—keep showing up.

Of course, there's also a risk in setting the bar too low. If, as a way to avoid disappointment (and possibly shame), you play it safe and don't expect much of yourself then it's more likely to work out, but it won't feel that uplifting when you pull it off. Plus you miss out on the greater benefits that come from shooting higher.

The goal here is to find the sweet spot that is something of a stretch but that you have a decent chance of pulling off. We can make this more likely by identifying your best ways of adopting new habits, so let's look to the past for some guidance. When you adopted new habits before, how did you set yourself up for success? Sure, other people were probably involved somehow, but what did you do that contributed to a positive outcome? What did others contribute that you can perhaps do this time? How did you keep at it? Are there existing habits or systems that can support this new habit? These might be the things to pay attention to and give yourself credit for doing now.

Finally, what is the benefit of making this change? In other words, what is it that makes all this fuss worthwhile? You want to keep that front and center when your motivation starts to sag, so what do you want to be sure to notice? This is the motivation that will pull you through that initial discomfort.

> This is a process. What's the next good thing you can do?

Put It to Work

- Notice when you get stuck on a negative thought about your performance—is it helpful or just making you feel bad? How does it affect what you do next?

- Today, notice three good things you did that helped your productivity. Were you surprised by any of them? How does noticing your successes affect what you do next?

- Really think about what is reasonable to expect of yourself in learning new productivity habits. Where do those ideas about habit change come from? Does your track record teach you anything useful about what to expect now? Or are the circumstances different now in important ways?

- **What, When, Where, and Why?**

What strategies are you going to apply from this chapter? How will this be different from what you're already doing? Or perhaps have done before?

When and where? The more specific you can be, the better. Then actively look for these moments. Or set an alarm or other reminder to pull your attention to it. How can you set things up beforehand to make this easier to stick with?

Why? What problem will this solve or improve? What are all the direct and indirect benefits of this change? How is your life better for it? This is your motivation for when you don't feel like it.

10. Surround Yourself with Good People

Unfortunately, ADHD can make you an easy target for others' disappointment and frustration, and potentially bad behavior.

We live, work, and interact with other people. We're affected by what they do and how they do it. It's reasonable, then, that we have expectations of others—and thoughts and feelings when they behave differently. That's not a license to behave badly, but opinions are free.

You deserve to be treated well. This shouldn't need to be said.

ADHD can make it harder to be the friend or coworker you want to be, to be consistent and predictable in the ways that others expect. This leave you feeling always behind, as if you owe others something. It's like a social debt. Others may see it this way as well. If your friend helps you move, you can buy them pizza and beer and then everything is balanced again. The problem with unmanaged ADHD is that it keeps racking up social debts so it never comes back to even.

All of this can create a situation where you tolerate borderline bad behavior and little digs because you feel as if you kind of deserve them. Or you may think you need to be the more accommodating friend or coworker to make up for those annoying ADHD moments. You don't. No one deserves bad behavior, but the emotions it brings up probably keep you from being on top of your game.

Build Your Cheering Section

We all need a little help from our friends. These are the people that we can be honest and vulnerable with, without fear of judgment. They get us.

If you tend to have too many negative or at least possibly judgmental experiences with people, then it's all the more important to have enough positive, supportive experiences as a counterbalance. This doesn't mean having friends that you never interrupt, forget to call back, or show up late for. As if. More like, these are people who appreciate all the rest of your good qualities. They don't need to love those ADHD moments, but they don't take it personally or define the friendship by them. You are more than your ADHD and these are the people who remind you of that. They see your hard work and good intentions and cheer you on even when you feel like you still fell short.

If you don't have enough of these people in your life, then make it an intentional project to find them. The easiest option is to promote some promising acquaintances to real friend status by extending your conversations with them and having more interactions. You may also need to expand your candidate pool. Where can you meet new people who might be a good fit for you? Find ways to show up—and then keep showing up so you can get to know people better. Put yourself out there more than you think you should—most people tend to assume that others are less interested in new friends than they actually are. At least show you're interested in a pleasant conversation and see where it goes from there.

Once you have some potential friends, earn their friendship by being a good friend yourself in ways that work well for you and without trying to be someone you're not. This might mean being honest and upfront about the ways that you may not meet their expectations. It's really important that you tell them your intentions, that you make clear you value them and want to be a good friend, but that sometimes your good intentions don't work out. Then give them permission to do the things that will make them happier in the friendship and to not worry about you taking offense—such as reaching out when they haven't heard from you in a while because you forgot to text back or reminding you (again) to return the item they lent you. This is especially important with new people who don't yet know you well enough to see through your actions to your good intentions.

Should They Be on Your Team?

You may have some people in your life who, let's just say, don't build you up. Some of these may be discretionary relationships like friends, whereas some may be relationships that are harder and messier to end, such as family or coworkers. No matter who you are, you won't like everyone and not everyone will like you. But some relationships may make you feel bad somehow, which then takes away from the rest of what you're doing. When that happens, you have a few options.

It might be helpful to have a conversation with the folks who don't get you, explaining the way ADHD affects your behavior in the relationship. Depending on how receptive they are, you may or may not want to say the word ADHD. I sometimes suggest talking about symptoms before diagnoses. In other words, say something like, "I work really hard at not interrupting, but I get excited and blurt something out before I realize it, so I am really sorry I cut you off." That way they don't assume you cut them off because you didn't care about the impact on them. I talk a lot more about whether or not to disclose your ADHD and, if so, how, in *33. Should You Tell People You Have ADHD?* and *34. What About Disclosing at Work?*

> People hope for good behavior but will often settle for good intentions.

Ultimately, you may decide that this relationship doesn't work for you, that it tends to make you feel worse. If you feel as if you've really put in the effort to make the desired changes and it still isn't enough, then it may be better to spend less time with this person or to keep things more superficial—or maybe to have no relationship at all. You're not required to stay in a situation that drags you down. Just as we sometimes need to edit down our to do list, sometimes we need to edit down our social list.

Put It to Work

- Notice those moments when ADHD impacts how you relate to others in your personal and professional lives. Does it affect what you expect or accept from other people? Do you put in effort to compensate for your ADHD—the right amount or too much?

- Identify at least one person in your life who builds you up. Think about what they do and how it affects you—really allow yourself to believe and feel their support and appreciation for who you are. (Bonus points: do the same for them.)

- Is there anyone in your life who perhaps needs a smaller role? If so, what is holding you back? Is there a part of you that agrees with the negative things that they say about you?

- ## What, When, Where, and Why?

What strategies are you going to apply from this chapter? How will this be different from what you're already doing? Or perhaps have done before?

When and where? The more specific you can be, the better. Then actively look for these moments. Or set an alarm or other reminder to pull your attention to it. How can you set things up beforehand to make this easier to stick with?

Why? What problem will this solve or improve? What are all the direct and indirect benefits of this change? How is your life better for it? This is your motivation for when you don't feel like it.

SECTION III. WHAT ARE YOU WORKING TOWARDS?

THE PURPOSE OF THIS BOOK is not simply getting more done—it's getting the *right* things done. It's putting most of your effort towards the most important goals. Aimless or misdirected activity isn't really that helpful. Part of productivity involves thinking before acting, which is hard for those who love the leaping more than the looking. This requires pausing for a moment to reflect and giving the executive functions time to do their thing. The payoff for jamming on the brakes to think for a sec is fewer dead ends, half-finished projects, and unnecessary detours.

You don't need to figure out the meaning of life, but you do need to have a few clear ideas about what is important to you and why—and what just feels like it's supposed to be important but you can never fully convince yourself that it is. This will make it much easier to fire up your motivation and clear a path through all those ideas that are kind of interesting, at least for a few minutes. Motivation is a precious and limited resource so you want to pour as much of it as possible into the goals that are most important to you.

Of course, there are often a number of ways to pursue those goals and accomplish the various tasks that will get you there. If you tend to get bored easily, you probably look for new ways to solve the same old problems. Or you're just a little too good at coming up with multiple ways to check a box. Having too many ideas is definitely better than being bored with nothing to do, but it does require some cognitive effort to sort through all those amazing ideas. The challenge is to keep your eye on the bigger goal you're working towards rather than jumping to solutions that don't match the problem or getting pulled off onto shiny side projects.

There is also the issue that your days are probably already fairly full, so you need to figure out what else you could realistically fit into those fast-moving twenty-four hours. Choosing means being clear on your big picture priorities and also on what you already have on deck. Then it becomes survival of the fittest.

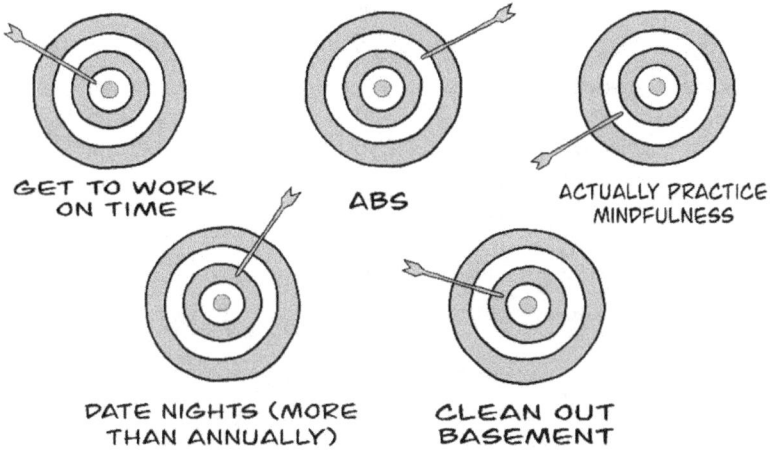

GET TO WORK
ON TIME

ABS

ACTUALLY PRACTICE
MINDFULNESS

DATE NIGHTS (MORE
THAN ANNUALLY)

CLEAN OUT
BASEMENT

11. What Are Your Goals? And Are They the Right Goals?

LIFE IS ONE MASSIVE JUGGLING act. We all have way more goals than time—personal development, professional, family, financial, health/fitness, home improvement, hobbies, streaming queues, the dream of an empty inbox, etc. This overabundance of goals guarantees hard choices of where to spend our finite budget of time and energy. Prioritizing is dynamic, constantly shifting, and always has loose ends. Life is messy and it's easy to feel like whatever we're doing isn't right.

To decide what is worth your time is not just about deciding whether a goal is worthy in its own right, but how it ranks relative to every other demand on your time. Balancing all of these competing and conflicting options is where it begins to feel like 3D chess. Meanwhile, the world is full of flashy distractions and temptations that

> What are you trying to do with your life? And why is this important to you?

definitely grab the attention in the moment, but probably don't add much to those bigger life goals. This is a universal challenge and no one feels 100% settled with whatever they decide to do.

When you have ADHD, it can feel as if you're always getting pulled by the next distraction and then scrambling to keep all the important balls in the air. Yet there's always the hope, for all of us, that we can somehow cram everything in, thereby avoiding having to really think about the kind of life that we want and therefore what does and doesn't make the cut.

Unfortunately, stealing from sleep doesn't invent more time—it just takes from tomorrow's productivity and mood. And multitasking just lets us pretend that we're doing more than we really are. No matter how you slice and dice it, we're still stuck with the same twenty-four hours, whether we're curing cancer or avoiding paperwork. The only exception here is that we can pay or otherwise get others to do things for us. This will take some tasks off of our to do list and perhaps make some goals more attainable—for example, hiring an accountant makes it easier to get our finances in order. I'm all in favor of paying others to do the things that we hate or suck at, but we still need to figure out how to make the best use of each day—and dollar.

Get Clear on Your Priorities

In all of this, we need to hold a balance between adding interesting new options (a fun new friend or hobby) and doing a good job on what's already on our plate. There's always the temptation to leap at novelty, especially when the status quo has challenges that make us uncomfortable or has just gone stale. There's something to be said for living a big life with lots of interesting goals, people, and activities. You will never have a dull moment, but you will probably also have a lot more stressful ones. On the other hand, there's also something to be said for living a smaller and more carefully curated life that will have less stress, but may also leave you feeling like you're missing out. To some extent, abundant and interesting will always be opposed to easy and comfortable. It's a personal decision of where on that spectrum you want to be at this point in your life— which may be different from what you preferred before or what you might want next. As your circumstances change, so might your preferences.

To the extent that you take the time to really think about what you want your life to look like now, you'll find you're more likely to have more moments where you're happy with your life. Sometimes this means you'll have to resist the temptation to impulsively leap at the next shiny thing. If you can hold for a minute, you can think about how this new option fits into your life and whether it's worth your time and energy. Of course, the more on top of your ADHD you are and the more your life is generally going OK, the easier it is to jam on the brakes before the tractor beam pulls you in. Yet another reason to really apply yourself to the rest of the chapters in the book.

The short questions with big implications are:

- What are you working towards in your life?

- Why are these goals important to you?

- How would your life be better for them?

- And, therefore, what are you *not* pursuing?

This can take real reflection and is really important, so take your time here. Think about what used to be important to you, why, and how you felt about it once you achieved those past goals. Think about what you wish for and what the hope is behind it. Maybe talk about it with the important people in your life. Do some journaling and see where your thoughts go. Reflect on it while out for a walk or run without your headphones.

Questions like these may also come up during times of transition as one big change pushes others, such as finishing school, getting a new job, starting or ending a relationship, having a baby, or moving. This can leave you feeling unmoored for a time or may bring stark clarity as your priorities fall into place.

In order to persist towards what is most important and not get hijacked by the next shiny idea that floats by, think of these big goals as your north star that helps you navigate through decisions. Keep that north star front and center, especially as distractions and demands from others threaten to pull you adrift.

Goals Should Drive Tasks

It's easy to be busy, but it can be much harder to figure out what is really worth working on. If you're not clear on what you're working towards, if everything is important, then you may bounce between tasks but not necessarily feel like you're making progress towards anything. In this case, it may feel like you're not productive enough, but the real problem is that you're spending too much time on activities that don't add enough value to your life. Ironically, being too busy to think tends to make you reactive to whatever demand pops up next—which keeps you too busy to think.

> Productivity begins with having the right goals. The right tasks follow from there.

Ideally, the things you do day by day should feel like they move your life forward in a personally meaningful way. Being clear on your goals makes it much easier to choose the tasks that are most likely to get you there. This is what separates being busy from being productive. Tasks are what you do; goals are why you do them. Tasks are the means; goals are the ends.

This clarity may be especially important if you have ADHD because it can be an important source of motivation when the task itself doesn't light you up. You can also remind yourself of the goal-related benefits of the boring task as a way to juice up your energy to work on it. Try to really feel, as vividly as possible, what you will get from this effort.

Dump the Duds

We all have goals that, if we were to be honest, get more lip service than action. Or maybe just a bunch of angst. Maybe they were more important before and they're still hanging on, or maybe they've just been loitering the whole time. This leads to all those tasks that we never get to—the stuff that clutters up the to do list or lurks at the edges of our mental list. We don't complete them, but we also don't cut them loose. This can look like a productivity problem, but it's really that this goal isn't enough of a priority to get much action.

If you never get to or finish a task, there are two possibilities and it's important to figure out which it is.

- **Procrastination** = your present self doesn't want to do it but your future self will want it to have been done

- **Not a priority** = your present self doesn't want to do it and your future self won't be that broken up about it

When we're procrastinating, there's a part of us that does care about the task. We may not want to do it now, but we do want the benefit of having done it. By contrast, if something isn't actually a priority, then we're not that invested in it, but we haven't yet made the decision to abandon it. Sure, some of these faltering goals may make a comeback (unlikely), but we may be better off just accepting that we aren't going to get to it. Light a candle if you need to. These false goals burn up mental energy every time we think about them and make us feel a little guilty about not making more progress.

It can get more emotionally complicated if you have a track record that is better at starting, or at least committing to, than you are at finishing. To cut something loose can feel like admitting defeat—yet another ball dropped, yet another promise broken. Keeping it on the to do list means that you don't need to officially admit you didn't do it. Or it can feel as if you *should* want to finish it, so maybe time will magically bestow interest upon you. Perhaps, but it comes at the cost of available mental energy for other, worthier goals.

> Our priorities are what we do, not what we say.

85

It's also possible that some of the goals that you don't make much progress on are actually other people's goals that you have only kind of agreed to take on. This can be really easy to do if you feel as if you drop the ball too often and that you kind of owe it to them to balance the relationship ledger. While all of that may be true, imposed goals are much harder to motivate for, especially if they're a bad fit in the first place. So, if it feels as if a goal is coming from someone else or may serve their needs more than your own, it's worth really thinking about whether you want to take it on and if you have the ability to complete it. If not, it may be best to pull the plug early and perhaps have an upfront conversation about it. You may not enjoy breaking the news, but most likely it will be less uncomfortable than what will happen later if you don't tell them and they find out in some other, more damaging way.

Having said that, we all do things that are much more important to someone else than to us. Sometimes we take one for the team. Generosity is a good thing. If it would be wise to complete this avoided task, then find a way to get it done, perhaps by reminding yourself of what kind of person you want to be in this relationship (rather than ruminating over how boring or annoying the task is).

I cover all of this in *35. Disappoint and Disagree with Grace.*

Put It to Work

- What would a good life look like now? (A short question that may need a lot of thought.)

- Are there some goals that you would be better off letting go, at least for now? Why do they not work for you now? What would it mean to let them go?

- Notice how you take on others' goals or are influenced by others' opinions. Do these goals work for you? Or do they better serve the other person? How do you balance these out?

- ## What, When, Where, and Why?

What strategies are you going to apply from this chapter? How will this be different from what you're already doing? Or perhaps have done before?

When and where? The more specific you can be, the better. Then actively look for these moments. Or set an alarm or other reminder to pull your attention to it. How can you set things up beforehand to make this easier to stick with?

Why? What problem will this solve or improve? What are all the direct and indirect benefits of this change? How is your life better for it? This is your motivation for when you don't feel like it.

12. Too Many Ideas! How to Sort Through All Your Options

HAVING A LOT OF IDEAS is a real strength—except when it feels overwhelming and hard choices need to be made to sort through all those gems. The more ideas you have, the more cognitive effort it takes to weigh them all against each other. You may be way better at that first part than the second part.

> Having a lot of ideas is a strength... except when it makes for a lot more work.

Speaking of effort, it can take effort to resist doing interesting things and also it takes effort to make ourselves do uninteresting things. ADHD makes both of those harder. Even much harder. No wonder you're so tired sometimes.

When you're letting your brainstorming run wild, you may want to pause and ask yourself, *Am I solving* this *problem or avoiding* that *one?* As in, sometimes it's way more fulfilling to try to figure out an interesting challenge that isn't actually central to what we need to do. Sure, it's related or maybe adjacent, but it's not exactly mission critical. Another way of thinking about it is, *Am I going* towards *something or* away *from something else?* If this resonates, you may want to check out *26. No, That's Fake Productivity.*

So, in the flurry of awesome ideas, these questions can focus you in:

- What problem are you trying to solve?
  - Does this idea solve the right problem in the best way?
  - Or is the real problem finding a way to make this task interesting enough to generate some motivation?
- What's the big picture?
  - How does this task relate to a bigger goal?
  - Does one option serve that bigger purpose better?
  - Or is it just novel and interesting?
  - Is a simpler (but less interesting) option actually better?

Sometimes it's hard to decide what to do because there isn't really a meaningful difference between the options. As in, each option is good in some ways, but the options are good in different ways, and are pretty much equally good in total. If you're trying to find a definitive winner, there isn't one. They all get the same grade. You may try to get out of this dilemma by coming up with a new option that will lead the pack and make the deciding easy. If you're feeling perfectionistic, you're going to make yourself nuts. In these situations, my vast experience and clinical wisdom leads me to give this advice: eeny, meeny, miney, moe. Seriously. Either you'll pick something and move on, or it will shake loose some stronger feelings about one of the options.

It may also be that you're just having fun with brainstorming and that the real thing you're doing here is having fun with the challenge of solving this puzzle. It's a creative intellectual exercise. This is totally fine if you're OK with not having an actionable plan yet—knock yourself out. This isn't failing at productivity; it's entertainment.

Maybe Good Enough is Good Enough

Sometimes the holdup isn't about sorting through relative merits, but rather reflects hesitation about committing to one idea. If you're worried that whatever option you choose won't go well, then you may be tempted to delay that moment of reckoning. This may be especially true if the task feels kind of ambiguous or you're not really sure what you're supposed to be doing or how it's supposed to end up. Without these parameters, it's easy to generate all sorts of ideas that conceivably could work, depending on what you're actually supposed to be doing. This brainstorming also feels as if you're doing something productive, which is kind of true, but not completely true.

In these cases, to really get something done, you probably need to go towards the discomfort rather than away from it. As in, accepting that it's uncomfortable to put your seal of approval on one idea over the others and potentially be judged for it. There's a point of diminishing returns where fiddling with the possibilities doesn't make you much more likely to choose the best answer and comes at the cost of everything else that you could be working on.

> Just because something feels uncomfortable doesn't mean that it's the wrong decision.

Having said that, if you really aren't sure of what you're supposed to be doing, then bite the bullet and find out. If you're worried that asking someone for clarification is going to reveal that maybe you missed it before, that's going to come out anyway when you don't give them what they asked for. It's almost always better to ask than guess wrong; usually the other person will appreciate your diligence in getting it right.

Same goes for running your options by someone else to get their input and help you decide, especially if this is a project you're doing for someone else. Their input is more helpful earlier than later since it will cut short some of those detours.

Put It to Work

- Notice when it takes effort to hold yourself back from pursuing an interesting idea. What are the situations that are the hardest to resist? When are you most vulnerable to getting hijacked by something shiny? What can you tell yourself to resist that delicious pull?

- Notice when you're picking an option just because it's more interesting. Is it actually the best option? What are you telling yourself to talk yourself into believing that this idea is the best one? How can you shoot down that sales pitch?

- What are you usually torn between when you just can't decide? What are you worried will happen? How do you eventually tip the balance?

- ## What, When, Where, and Why?

What strategies are you going to apply from this chapter? How will this be different from what you're already doing? Or perhaps have done before?

When and where? The more specific you can be, the better. Then actively look for these moments. Or set an alarm or other reminder to pull your attention to it. How can you set things up beforehand to make this easier to stick with?

Why? What problem will this solve or improve? What are all the direct and indirect benefits of this change? How is your life better for it? This is your motivation for when you don't feel like it.

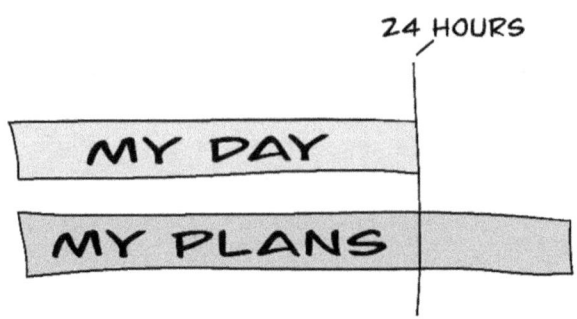

13. Do You Actually Have Time for That?

AS SOMEONE WHO TENDS TO take a lot on, I am acutely aware of time and how it so easily gets filled. As a result, all sorts of things are doable in theory... except for everything else I'm already doing.

Therefore, taking on new projects needs to be survival of the fittest. This means asking ourselves, *What makes this project worth doing?* If you had to explain it to a friend or coworker, could you make a convincing case? Could you convince a jury? Or your romantic partner without getting that look? (You know the look.) Here's a bit of advice: If you can connect this project to some bigger goal, like I discussed in *11. What Are Your Goals? And Are They the Right Goals?*, you will probably be more convincing.

In theory, I have time for everything. In reality, I have time for nothing.

Time is always zero sum (ultimately).

Before you promote this new project to the top of your to do list, you should probably pause for a second to think about (or, preferably, look up) what else is happening and needs to be completed and by when. It's easy to just prove that this project has some merits—lots of things do. What's harder is to explain why your time is better spent here than it is on whatever project that you now don't have time for. Deciding what no longer makes the cut may take some real thought. Is this new project good enough to beat out something else? Or is it just kind of interesting right now? If you have ADHD, you're really good at finding interesting activities. This can be a blessing and a curse.

I certainly don't want to suggest that you need to be a relentless productivity robot. It's totally fine to do stuff just because it's fun or interesting. We need that, too. My point here is to be honest about it. If something is mostly just interesting but not actually that useful, then don't try to convince yourself it is so that you don't have to feel guilty for procrastinating on more important tasks. You may also want to ask yourself if you could convince your future self that it's worth doing because you're definitely going to face their judgment. That bullet can't be dodged. (Unless you forget about it.) The real measure of your decision-making is how you will feel about it afterwards. If you will regret it, then remind yourself of how that regret feels, as vividly as possible, to help you push away the temptation. If your future self would be cool with it, then dive in and enjoy.

Yes, You Do Have Time

We all have situations where we say that we didn't do something because we didn't have time. Sounds like a good reason. But if we were 100% honest, it's that we chose to do other things that we needed or wanted to do more, so there wasn't enough time *left over* for the task that we didn't do. In other words, it didn't make the cut. Here's the proof: if your house was on fire, you wouldn't say that you didn't have time to grab your prized possessions and run to safety because you had *so many* emails... As soon as you smelled smoke, your priorities would shift.

I'm not saying this to call everyone a liar (even though we all are). Rather, it's empowering to see that we do have the ability to make choices about where we put our time and how we set our priorities. Some tasks will make the cut and others won't. Fine. Let's own that agency. Saying that we didn't have time makes

> "Sorry, I didn't have time," is the intersection of the twenty-four day and politeness.

it sound as if it was something that happened to us, rather than a situation that we created and maybe even wanted. It feeds a narrative that we don't control our actions or destiny. It's easy to feel like this if you aren't managing your ADHD well, so feeling more in charge of your life is one of the big goals here.

Sometimes the task that we didn't get to was self-imposed and we only need to wrestle with our own conscience about it. Of course, sometimes saying that we didn't have time is more of a social nicety that goes over better than telling someone that we just didn't want to do it. As admirable as honesty is, there's definitely a point where honest begins to overlap with asshole, so we need to consider that, too. When you're being polite to someone else, try to remind yourself that you're making choices here. And that the other person may know the truth of what happened and is also being polite. Don't ask, don't tell.

Manage Others' Requests

Unfortunately, we can't always take a pass on what others ask of us, no matter how politely we say we don't have time and how much they pretend to believe us. If a task is coming from someone else, then it gets even more complicated because you need to also consider how important it is to them—and how important their importance is to you. Your boss's happiness may be more important than a coworker's. Even if it's your boss, if you have other commitments you may still need to say that you don't have time to do what they're asking, or at least that they then need to decide which of your other tasks gets cut. In order to be assertive, you may need to find a way to be OK with their disappointment (or worse). Where it gets messy with ADHD is when you feel as if you disappoint them too often and therefore can't say no to this request, even if it's reasonable to do so.

If the request is stressing you out too much, start by asking questions before feeling like you have to say yes. How important is this to them? Why? What is their preferred deadline? What is the real deadline? Where can they be flexible? Again, if you already feel as if you're on thin ice, you may not feel like you can ask these questions. Perhaps, but there's an important difference between asking questions to find out how to best please this person versus trying to weasel out of work. If you have good intentions, it's better to take a minute to find out if there is a way to make this more likely to work out.

You may also want to be clear about the timing you can pull off and what might get in your way. Again, if you have a reputation for missing deadlines, you may feel like you don't have the right to talk about possible delays. If anything, it's more important to set the right expectations right from the beginning so the other person doesn't later assume that you just dropped the ball. You may also want to clarify whether you will let them know that you're running late or whether they should check in with you. If it's your boss, then probably you should let them know. If you're doing someone else a favor, then that ball's probably in their court.

A lot of productivity involves coordinating with other people, especially when you have ADHD, so I have an entire section on it: *VII. The Social Side of Productivity*. If other people's expectations, opinions, and judgments keep you up at night, I've got your back.

Time Is Money, Money Is Time

While it's true that we can't create more time, we can free up some space in our schedules by converting money into time. As in, you can pay someone to do what you don't want to—whether it's changing your oil, cleaning your house, or making lunch—leaving you with time for other pursuits. Hopefully this is an intentional choice, but there is also the ADHD tax, which is all the ways that your ADHD forces you to spend more money to undo its impact, such as paying more for shipping because you forgot to order it earlier, late fees, buying replacement items because you either lost or can't find the original, buying lunch when you ran out of time to make something, etc. While the money spent feels better than the crummy alternative, there are definitely more rewarding ways to spend that money. Of course, if you're more efficient and on top of things, then you won't need to convert money into time as often.

> Good strategies are deductible from the ADHD tax.

We can also run this the other way and convert time into money by working more or doing things ourselves which leaves money for other goals. Again, this is good if it feels like an intentional choice, but it may be a hard necessity if you spent too much money in other places or just don't have the extra.

Among all the other potential benefits that you may get from working hard with this book, you may also find that it improves how you spend money and how you feel about where that money goes.

Put It to Work

- How does it tend to work out when you take on something interesting that you don't actually have time for? How do you shoot down the reasons for why you don't have time? How can you remind yourself of this when that situation comes up?

- How is it helpful when you know what else you need to do when a new potential task comes up? How does this change how you think about this new task? (Hint: This is your motivation to keep your schedule and to do list up to date.)

- What can you tell yourself to feel better about saying no to a request from someone else? What's the fear of what would happen? How likely is it? How can you politely but firmly explain to them why you won't be doing what they ask?

• What, When, Where, and Why?

What strategies are you going to apply from this chapter? How will this be different from what you're already doing? Or perhaps have done before?

When and where? The more specific you can be, the better. Then actively look for these moments. Or set an alarm or other reminder to pull your attention to it. How can you set things up beforehand to make this easier to stick with?

Why? What problem will this solve or improve? What are all the direct and indirect benefits of this change? How is your life better for it? This is your motivation for when you don't feel like it.

SECTION IV. SET UP A GOOD WORK ENVIRONMENT

HAVING ADHD MAKES FOR A MORE direct connection to the world around you. Whatever happens around you slides into your attention more easily and more deeply. Same for all those random thoughts and feelings inside your own head and body. There's less of a filter to keep out some of these inputs, like the scratching of your classmate's pencil on her paper while the teacher was apparently announcing the test. This makes it that much more important to be intentional about the situations you put yourself into and how you set yourself up for success.

I jokingly say that my superpower is impatience. My wife doesn't think that's nearly as hilarious as I do, but I think it's what makes me so attuned to the productivity challenges associated with ADHD. I've chilled out some over the decades, but I hate wasting time or when things take longer than they should. I have a lot I want to do, so I want to work efficiently, especially on the boring stuff, so I can get to the good stuff. A lot of this involves creating a workspace where it takes less effort to get the job done. The best part is that setting things up ahead of time (e.g., putting your phone out of reach) involves doing the right thing only once, versus trying to resist distractions and temptations that require us to make the right decision every single time. I don't like those odds...

That's what this section is about—shaping the world around you so that your internal mental machinery works better. This obviously involves reducing distractions that pull you away, but it also involves the flip side of avoiding the situations where you get stuck too long. Good attention regulation involves sticking when you should stick and shifting when you should shift. A good work environment nudges you in the right direction at the right moment.

It would be hard to write a book on ADHD and productivity without covering how to manage screens, but I did succeed in writing half of one before addressing this glaring topic. Our screens are easy to love and also easy to hate, probably more so if you have ADHD. They're also inescapable, so let's find a way to coexist.

Part of a good workspace is having the right amount of stuff and in generally the right places. Folks with ADHD tend to hold on to more than they really need, not because they love it all, but because no one breaks in in the middle of the night to steal all the extra crap that they don't need. Oh yeah, and because going through your stuff is really boring and hope burns eternal on that break-in plan. Unfortunately, all that extra stuff can be like sand in the gears of the well-oiled machine that you dream your productivity can be.

Clearing the decks a bit is just part of what it takes to create a good workflow, but that workflow is a thing of beauty when you get it set up. Swiss precision may be overly ambitious, but let's at least sand down the rough spots.

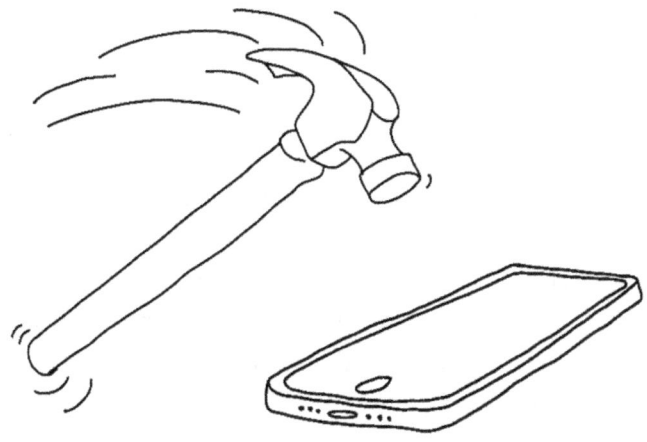

14. Get the Distractions Before They Get You

A LOT OF MANAGING ADHD is about managing your environment because ADHD makes it harder to resist distractions and temptations. They pull harder on your attention and feelings and which then influence your actions. One way to think about it is that ADHD makes you slower to jam on the mental brakes before your attention shifts. Away we go! Everyone's attention gets hijacked sometimes, but folks without ADHD can hit the brakes a little quicker and therefore have an extra moment to consider what to do next, including to ignore that distraction or temptation.

Therefore, rather than counting on your attention's ability to resist distractions, it's more effective to tweak the external environment so there are fewer pings on your attention in the first place. It takes a little drop of willpower to pull your attention back and push away the temptation—no big deal until too much has dripped away. Then you're much more likely to not resist the next one. The goal is to kill the competition by making distractions less frequent, noisy, interesting, intense, or close.

Of course, we all like to think that we will be able to resist those distractions so that we don't have to do anything different. It takes some effort to actively and preemptively manage distractions, so we may prefer to just plow ahead instead and hope for the best. Fingers crossed! Or we may kind of know that we need to put our phone away, for example, but we like having it there so we talk ourselves into why it's OK. Of course, given our track record, it would probably be really hard to talk anyone else into believing that it will be OK, which is why we don't ask anyone else. This is another one of those situations where you can do whatever you want—it's your life so it's your choice. Seriously. The way that I would think about it is how you will feel afterwards. If you perhaps get distracted but you're fine with it, then it's fine. But if you would later regret it, then I would hope that you made a different choice. You probably don't need more regret.

Having had a lot of conversations about productivity, I find that managing attention well is a foundation for managing time well. Or, as the conversations usually start, not managing attention well tends to tank all those grand time management plans. This is especially important in really distracting environments. Also, if you don't take medication or if your meds have worn off, you will be more vulnerable to distractions.

> Managing time begins with managing attention. Which begins with managing your environment.

So, the question to you is: What does a good work environment look like for you? Really think about it. It may be that the environment that you're actually most productive in is not the one that you usually work in. It may also vary a lot by the type of task or time of day. As I've said before, you don't need to be a relentless productivity robot. It's totally fine to take the more leisurely route. But when you really want to crank stuff out, how can you set yourself up to be most effective?

If you work around other people, you may need to explain your preferred methods so they don't jump to the wrong conclusions. For example, using earbuds doesn't mean that you're asocial. Nor is asking to use the conference room to really spread out and immerse yourself in a complex project. Just explain the productivity benefits and most people will be fine. And if they do get judgey, then that probably tells you more about them than about you.

Work It from Both Sides

Attention is all about competition, as I discussed in *3. ADHD Makes It Harder to Feel the Future*. Every stimulus in that moment competes for your attention, but we can only pay attention to a few things at a time. Actually, really only to one thing at a time, but we can quickly jump back and forth between a few things so it feels as if we're paying attention to all of them. If something new comes in, something old has to get bumped out. The hope in each moment is that we will be paying attention to the most important thing and ignoring the rest.

I find it useful to think of this as a signal-to-noise ratio where we want the signal to be louder than the noise so that it is more likely to get grabbed by our attention. The signal is what we want to pay attention to, and the noise is everything else that is competing for our attention. This gives us two potential clusters of strategies. A lot of ADHD-friendly strategies involve making the signal louder— things like alarms, various reminders, whiteboards, checklists, scribbled notes, body doubling, etc. On the flip side of the coin, we can also make the noise quieter—noise-cancelling earbuds, white noise, clearing clutter, muting notifications, asking not to be interrupted, etc. By thinking about both sides of this, we're more likely to help the signal win out over the noise.

Put It to Work

- Notice how simple distractions cost you time and productivity. How little does it take sometimes to steal away your focus? How long can it take to get back to where you were?

- Dial down one of your most disruptive distractions and notice how it affects your productivity. How much easier is it to stay focused? How much longer do you work before taking a break?

- Set up your best work environment for one of your hardest tasks and notice how productive you are. How different is this from what you can do in your standard work environment? How do you feel about that difference?

- ## What, When, Where, and Why?

What strategies are you going to apply from this chapter? How will this be different from what you're already doing? Or perhaps have done before?

When and where? The more specific you can be, the better. Then actively look for these moments. Or set an alarm or other reminder to pull your attention to it. How can you set things up beforehand to make this easier to stick with?

Why? What problem will this solve or improve? What are all the direct and indirect benefits of this change? How is your life better for it? This is your motivation for when you don't feel like it.

15. Stay Away from Where You Get Stuck or Slide Away

I SOMETIMES ADVISE CLIENTS TO STAY away from sticky or slippery activities. That sounds dirty, but unfortunately isn't. It's about where your attention sticks or slips. Some activities are sticky, meaning that it's too easy to get stuck on them, whether in full hyperfocus or just spending more time than you would want to. For example, a lot of online content is made to be sticky through all sorts of subtle and not so subtle ways that keep us engaged—plus all the ways that draw us back to be stuck again. But any activity that you really enjoy has the potential to be sticky because obviously you will want to spend more time on it and it will take mental effort to pull yourself away. Plus, the more you're in the flow, the easier it is to not realize how long you've been at it.

By contrast, some activities are slippery, meaning that it's too easy to slip off onto other activities. This is more about distractibility and involves anything that too easily slides you over to another activity. Checking email is a prime example—one or two clicks and you're gone. Or running into a store to grab one thing and then coming out with a bunch more and much later than planned. The more that's going on in a place or activity and the more enticing it is, the more mental effort it takes to keep the core mission in working memory and ignore everything else (look away, not that, keep moving).

Once our attention is stuck or has slipped away, it's much harder to wrangle our attention to where it would be most useful. Sometimes the stuckness or slippery side mission has to run its course before we even realize what happened. This might be a minute or... well, much more. There's also the risk of just plain forgetting what else we should have done until the forgotten task comes screeching back into awareness. (Oh no!)

Because we don't fully realize when we're sticking or slipping, the point of intervention is before starting these time stealers. Once you're a couple steps in and your attention has been hijacked, it's much, much harder to swing it around. It's kind of like how the time to decide to not eat fifty potato chips is before you eat the first one, not after—that first one almost guarantees the second. Or better yet, before you're even looking at the bag. And best of all, before you even turn down that aisle in the supermarket.

If your track record is pretty clear on how certain things end (if I do A then I usually do B), then it's important to be honest with yourself about it. The reason why it's important is not that someone else might judge you for it, but because you yourself will regret it later. Life has enough regrets already without adding to the pile. Don't set yourself up for trouble by pretending that things will work out differently if there are no good reasons to support that optimism. Now if, in this situation, you're OK with getting stuck or slipping away, then that's a different story—probably no regrets there. Go for it.

> Do whatever you want—just be honest about it. It's worth it if it's worth it.

Of course, grudgingly admitting that it's probably a good idea to stay away from sticky and slippery activities is a lot easier than actually staying away or setting up barriers to keep them farther away. The pull of temptation can be really strong. It can help to remind yourself of the cost of getting sucked away and also the benefits of staying on track with your plans. How good will it feel to keep getting things done? Picture yourself in an hour or two after you stayed on track. Maybe even tell yourself out loud how great that would be.

The tricky part with this is that we like to think that we can just dip into something and then pull ourselves out because that way we can justify that fun sticky or slippery activity. Once in a while it actually works out well, so we like to think that this will be one of those times even if the odds are stacked against it. Therefore, it's important to be really honest with yourself about how likely it is to work out well. If you had to make a bet about it, if you had to throw down fifty bucks, would you take that bet?

So, here's a suggestion (and possibly a challenge). The next time you're talking yourself into defying the odds with one of these activities, pull out some money and lay it out in front of you. Look at those bills while you explain to yourself why this is going to work out well. This might make it more real. Do you still feel confident? Confident enough to give that money away if it doesn't work out?

Are You Setting Up Later Trouble?

I've noticed that sometimes people preemptively let themselves off the hook later by what they do or don't do earlier. They quietly or subtly decide to tilt the odds of what will happen later. For example, if you don't set an alarm and then get onto sticky social media, it isn't really that surprising that you then forget to make that dreaded phone call on time. But this way you can say that you simply forgot (whoops!), which perhaps feels better than saying that you chose to not make the call. It maintains some plausible deniability since we all forget things sometimes.

> Just because we convince ourselves of something doesn't mean that we actually believe it.

This is different from those times when you really did intend to do something but your attention got hijacked by something else—that difference between knowing and doing that we keep talking about.

The reason why this distinction matters is that there's a part of us that knows that we're not being honest, whether just with ourselves or with someone else. We know we're not being the person that we want to be. If you have too many of these moments, it can really affect your self-esteem and hopes for improvement.

If you realize that you're letting yourself off the hook, ask yourself, *Is there something about the avoided task that makes me uncomfortable?* It's fine to admit that you don't want to do it and that you're tempted to avoid it. No shame there. But even if it makes you uncomfortable, it would probably still be better to make a conscious decision on whether or not you are going to do the task. Honestly assess the costs and benefits and whether you're up for it. If you want to talk yourself into doing it, then really remind yourself of how the gains will be worth the suffering. Or maybe try to think of a less uncomfortable way to do it. If you just can't talk yourself into doing it, then be honest about that rather than tricking yourself into believing that you will. The task probably isn't getting done anyway, but at least this way you can feel good about making a real decision about it.

You may also want to check out *24. Just Bite the Bullet on Things You Hate.*

Put It to Work

- Identify your stickiest and slipperiest activities—how hard is it to break away once you start? How long do you tend to spend on them compared to how long you want to think you will?

- How can you set up barriers to your stickiest and slipperiest activities? When are you most vulnerable to these activities? How can you convince yourself to avoid the first steps towards them? What are the justifications that will be the hardest to resist?

- Notice how you set up later trouble through the choices that you (implicitly) made earlier. How can you remind yourself to make a real decision instead?

- **What, When, Where, and Why?**

What strategies are you going to apply from this chapter? How will this be different from what you're already doing? Or perhaps have done before?

When and where? The more specific you can be, the better. Then actively look for these moments. Or set an alarm or other reminder to pull your attention to it. How can you set things up beforehand to make this easier to stick with?

Why? What problem will this solve or improve? What are all the direct and indirect benefits of this change? How is your life better for it? This is your motivation for when you don't feel like it.

16. Control the Screens Before They Control You

I T'S KIND OF SHOCKING THAT it took me until halfway through a book on ADHD productivity before addressing screentime. In my defense, people got distracted and screwed around long before screens ruled our lives, so it's not just about the glowing menace.

Understandably, we all tend to have a love/hate relationship with our devices. I'm going to riff on a very old line from *The Simpsons*: screens—the cause of, and solution to, many of productivity's problems. Tech-based solutions abound, and some of them aren't even related to countering tech-based problems.

What makes it worse is that because our devices are so integrated into every aspect of our lives, we work and play in the same place, so it takes even more planning and self-restraint to not get distracted into deep dives. It literally can take less than a second to click or toggle over to something that is definitely more interesting than what we're supposed to be doing. A flash of impulse leads to a distracted loss of time awareness and then you might as well set fire to your to do list.

Granted, we are all responsible for our actions, but also the cards are stacked against us. Online content is optimized for maximum viewing time. It actively and passively draws us back. (You should definitely Google this if you don't believe me. There are some really interesting and time consuming articles with lots of other links where you can read all about it. And about all sorts of unrelated topics.) ADHD makes it harder to resist—and easier to lose track of time. So much of our screen time is kind of reflexive, where we grab our phone or toggle over to a different tab without even really thinking about it. All those little bits can really add up. If you find it helpful to be slightly horrified, look up your total screen time and specifically where that time goes. Yikes!

> I love my wife, but sometimes I leave the house without her.
>
> *– Stephen Colbert, talking about his cell phone*

Part of the problem is that screens are easy palate cleansers as we go from one activity to another. It's a natural time to check in on messages of various kinds, news, notifications, new content, etc. Makes sense—some of it might be helpful to know. It just becomes a problem when we do it too often. I challenge clients sometimes by saying that unless you drive the ambulance, you don't need to be immediately available. It can probably wait.

There's also the fact that screens are a great path of least resistance that is easier and more fun than that activity that we're not yet up for dealing with. There's the added bonus that if you're checking your email or texts, then you can justify it because you're being responsive (you should probably also read some articles about that, too). It's harder to make it into a virtue when you're checking social media, but maybe... And if you're checking the news then you're being an informed citizen which I think they said was important in that sophomore social studies class.

Use Your Screens Intentionally

It's not my place to tell you how much time to spend on your screens. That's for you to figure out. And your romantic partner to have opinions about. I'm also not going to say that screen time is inherently bad. From the perspective of this book, it comes down to how it affects your productivity and how you feel about that. The goal here isn't to be a relentless productivity robot. It's important also to have cognitively easy time where we don't have to think too hard or push ourselves to stay on task. Screens can be great for that. The tricky part with screens is that we're often not aware of how much time we spend on them and how much they occupy our thoughts even when we're not on them.

Like many things in life, we're more likely to be happy later if we have some sort of a plan for what we're doing. Just going with the flow gives the universe more influence over your fate than probably most people would want. When it comes to screens, it's almost guaranteed that without some sort of a plan, you will tend to spend more time than you would want—possibly a lot more. This then leaves you regretting how much time you spent online and feeling very differently afterward than you did at the time.

Maybe I'm picky, but my big complaint about too much of what's online is that it's kind of interesting. You know, not amazing, but OK. Interesting enough to stay on it, but not so great that you really remember it the next day. This is fine if you're killing time standing in line, but there are so many other, better ways to spend chunks of time that have better payoffs. Too many of these opportunities get soaked up by content that's merely so-so. Maybe there's a subgoal here to try to limit yourself to really good content and to move on to other things if it's just OK.

> The algorithms and people who create them are smarter than the rest of us.

Ask yourself the question, What's important to me that I don't have enough time for? Then ask yourself the question, How much more time would I have if I spent less on OK content?

If you really want to do something about this, then let's talk about how to reduce the pull that screens have on your attention and time. As I've talked about before, the least effective solution is to rely on willpower to resist temptation. This works just as well for screens as it does for cookies. Maybe worse. Much more effective is to reduce how large a temptation looms in your attention by making it quieter or putting it farther away. Some obvious strategies that you already know:

- Silence your phone and turn off notifications

- Place phone face down so you can't see the notifications

- Unsubscribe from content that's just not that good

- Put your phone out of reach—the farther, the better

You can also reduce how often you dive into your phone by creating a small speed bump that slows down using your phone so it becomes less reflexive and more intentional:

- Put a rubber band on your phone so you need to pull it off first or work around it (this is just annoying enough to actually work)

- Put your phone on airplane mode or turn it off completely so you need to wait to connect

- Reduce the notifications that get through, especially if you're trying to get other stuff done

- Use a long and annoying password to unlock your phone

- Close out tabs or delete apps so it's more work to get that content

- Again, place your phone farther away so it's a hassle to get it

- Use an app that promotes time off your phone, then get crazy competitive about it

Once you're on your phone, there's also the question of how long you spend. Just as relying on raw willpower tends to not work that well, relying on your innate ability to track how long you've been on your phone is probably also not going to work out that well. Again, it's just like with cookies where eating one makes it easier to eat another without making a specific, conscious decision to do so. Therefore, the best way to not spend too long online is to not get on in the first place. The next best way is to create some sort of a break in the action so you can notice how long it's been and maybe then decide to get off. This sounds good in theory, but you also need to be honest with yourself about how likely that is to actually work out.

For example, you could:

- Set a timer

- Look at your phone standing up so it's less comfortable

- Look at your phone before you have to do something else so there's a hard stop—this is risky, so use with caution

- Only look at something specific on your phone and don't even think about jumping over to something you spend too long on (fingers crossed!)

None of these strategies for managing phone time are a guarantee, but they give you an extra moment to make a different choice. It's all about trying to squeeze in a little conscious choice in the place of knee-jerk reflex. As I talked about in *6. What Exactly Is Getting in Your Way Here?*, these strategies involve some planning to increase awareness, but they don't really do anything for motivation—you still have to choose to walk away from the enjoyable screen. This probably involves reminding yourself of the benefits of what else you could be doing, even though it will be less fun in the moment.

And, since we're not 100% rational decision makers, you may also need some of the more advanced strategies below.

Maybe It's Emotional

In addition to the primarily cognitive strategies above, there may also be more emotional reasons at play when we slide off into easy distractions. For example, are you:

- Stressed out, feeling depleted, and need a recharge?

- Anxious and uncertain about how to tackle the next project?

- Pretty sure you won't do a good job on that next project?

- Resentful about what you should be working on?

- Worried about social fallout from what you do or don't do on social media?

These aren't necessarily about ADHD, but they can exacerbate any other struggles with productivity. So, pay attention to when, where, and why you dive off into online content that's emotionally easier—and spend much longer on than you should. What's happening there? How do you feel in that moment? What are you hoping to feel instead?

If there are emotional reasons driving this, then just setting an alarm or using the other strategies above probably isn't going to do the trick. Instead, you need to work on other ways of managing those feelings. Hopefully the rest of this book will help you feel more on top of your life, but if you still feel as if you're struggling more than you should, you may want to talk to a therapist. Life is hard enough without that extra layer.

Do You Need an Internet Blocker? Or Cell Phone Lockbox?

When someone has trouble limiting how much they drink, the obvious advice is to remove alcohol from the house and to stay away from bars. If you're unable to manage your alcohol with willpower, then you need to use more external limits. The same advice applies to managing online content if you tend to overdo it.

As for when too much is too much, that's something you need to decide for yourself. I take the position that the proof is in the pudding: Are you looking up pudding recipes when you should be working? How do you feel before, during, and after time online? If you continue to feel bad about how much time you spend online, or at least how much other stuff you're (not) getting done, then maybe you would be better off making some changes. If the changes you've tried aren't getting the job done (internet 10, you 0), then you may need to bite the bullet on some stronger interventions.

The fact that internet blockers exist tells you that you're not alone. Also, not one of those blockers uses the word ADHD in their marketing materials, so it's not only an ADHD problem. These are apps or browser extensions that can limit your total time online, as well as track total time spent for specific platforms or within categories (e.g., all social media). You can also set blackout times, as in midnight – 8 AM. Ideally, their time tracking works across browsers and devices (phone,

> The internet is the land that time forgot and where good plans come to die.

laptop, tablet). They are much more robust than whatever is built into the OS that can be easily swiped away and ignored. Usually, they work best if someone else has admin rights and can set the parameters (and not impulsively reset them). The obvious market for these is parents, but adults have just as much need. Maybe more, since no one is looking over our shoulders.

There are also a variety of different cell phone lockboxes available that will make your phone inaccessible for a programmed amount of time. The better ones still allow you to swipe to answer a call so you're not completely inaccessible—or able to use that as an excuse to not lock away your phone. Your Bluetooth earbuds should still work so you will still have that benefit. If you're someone who has good willpower at the start of a work session but finds it crumbling when things get boring, then this could be just the tool for you. You still need to make those good choices in those early moments, but then your phone's fate is sealed—literally and figuratively. And it's much more reliable than hoping you get mugged.

As we all know, where there is a will, there's a way to circumvent these restrictions, so if you're looking for the 100% solution then you should probably smash your phone. Or, if you're just saying it isn't 100% to justify not doing anything at all, then remind yourself that your current 6% solution of relying on willpower isn't exactly crushing it. There is not one single solution in this book that will force you to do what you don't want to do. You still need to decide and then commit. But if you are willing to put in the effort, then you have a shot at it.

If you continue to spend too much time online but resist using more effective tools or strategies, then you need to ask yourself why. Or, if you're in my office, I will ask you why. What's the hesitation? And if you aren't going to use something to limit online time, then what's the alternative that will work better? Or do you need to change your goals? If so, that's totally fine. You get to decide what you do. Where this becomes a problem is when your actions and your stated goals don't line up because you will then regret it and get down on yourself. We can probably all agree that we don't want that.

Ultimately, if the internet continues to undo your grand plans, then it comes down to this question: What are your goals and what are you willing to do to get there? You may need to really think about that one.

Put It to Work

- Really think about your time online—what improves your life or takes away from it? At what point does that flip over? What do you want that balance to be?

- What barriers to junk screentime would work best for you? How do you talk yourself out of using them? What could you tell yourself to really remind yourself of what you could be doing instead?

- Measure your time on various platforms and compare against your preferred time. How do you feel about this difference? What else could you do with that additional time? Is now maybe the time to take stronger action?

- ## What, When, Where, and Why?

What strategies are you going to apply from this chapter? How will this be different from what you're already doing? Or perhaps have done before?

When and where? The more specific you can be, the better. Then actively look for these moments. Or set an alarm or other reminder to pull your attention to it. How can you set things up beforehand to make this easier to stick with?

Why? What problem will this solve or improve? What are all the direct and indirect benefits of this change? How is your life better for it? This is your motivation for when you don't feel like it.

17. Do You Really Need to Keep That?

WHERE DID ALL THIS STUFF come from? And is it OK to secretly wish for a fire to just burn up all the extra stuff?

If you have ADHD and you aren't managing it well, it's probably going to leave some visible traces in your life. And in your wake. Items come into our lives, stick around, then leave. Having ADHD can impact all three of those phases. Impulsive purchases can bring extra stuff in, as can buying replacements for the items that you can't currently find. Or forgot you own.

As we use items, they need to get put back where they belong, whether it's laundry, paperwork to be saved, cooking items, hobbies, etc. ADHD makes it harder to get everything back to where it belongs. Procrastinating and then rushing doesn't leave time to clean up behind you ("I was totally going to put this all away"). Of course, this also presumes that you have a clear organizational system for where things go—and that there isn't a bunch of other stuff in the way that makes it too frustrating to use.

Because going through your stuff to cull out what you no longer need is pretty boring (OK, *really* boring), it kind of never happens. Having too much stuff makes it impossible to get organized. As I say, you can't organize six gallons of water into a five-gallon bucket. So, the disorganization just gets worse as even more things accumulate. At this point, it's much more work to put things where they belong and too easy to feel as if one more thing won't make it any worse. This is the disorganization death spiral.

It's also tempting to keep things just in case you need them later. This is especially true if you're not entirely sure about what you need to keep and have a general fear of making the wrong decision (you know, on account of all those wrong decisions). Sometimes we're not specifically deciding to keep something so much as we're not really deciding either way, but we put it aside with the idea that we will figure it out later. Sometimes this is reasonable, but it leads to a lot of extra stuff when we kick too many cans down the road and then wonder where the hell all these cans came from.

> Clutter is deferred decisions.

Finally, we also keep things with the hope that, someday, we will use it. Oh, the projects I will do!

It's hard to bite the bullet on tackling all that clutter because it creates a small daily cost that's annoying but (mostly) not terrible, whereas doing the big cleanup is terrible right now. It's pretty easy to pick the preferable option there.

Clear the Piles, Get More Done

As you probably know quite well, all this extra stuff can trip up your productivity. There's a cost in not finding what you need when you need it. All that extra stuff means time lost looking for things. Plus, it's distracting and breaks the flow, which may not be easy to dial back in, especially if you get caught up in a side project.

I will admit that I tend to be a minimalist and that everyone else doesn't need to feel the same way. And I'm sure as hell not making this a moral issue or adding any judgment. But when your stuff brings you more stress than joy, you may want to cut some loose. I won't say that this is easy and it definitely isn't fun. It may take some real cognitive and emotional effort to figure out what to keep or toss and how to put it all away. My friend Chrstine Hargrove, PhD suggests pretending you're going through someone else's stuff—there's less emotional attachment so it's easier to just "be rational" about it all.

There are many ways to be organized, but if you tend to struggle with this, then I suggest you focus on functionality first— whatever helps you manage the rest of your life best. Being organized is a means to an end. Focus on whatever is going to have the biggest impact on your productivity, ADHD management, and general happiness.

> Each new item adds value to your life... until it starts subtracting from it.

However you organize your stuff, my strong advice is to first get rid of as much as you can. Start where you can make the biggest difference the quickest so you have something to show for your effort. Then notice that progress and give yourself some credit. As you consider what to do with something, ask yourself, *How likely am I to actually need or use this?* Decide quickly, without over-thinking, with a bias towards getting rid of it, especially the old stuff. The longer you think about something, the more you will talk yourself into all the reasons why you should keep it. With rare exceptions, don't let yourself defer deciding—make a choice and move on. If you're not sure what you need to keep, such as paperwork for taxes, then do the research to find out.

You may feel as if your disorganization is so bad that it has become insurmountable—and shame inducing. It may be completely overwhelming so you can't even think about it without sweating. Or it would take so long to get through it all that you would only have enough time for it if you were placed on house arrest. Even then, you might prefer to chew your way through the front door than to slog through it all. Fortunately, a professional organizer can help in all these situations. They can help you plow through the backlog more quickly and painlessly, as well as create better systems to manage your stuff going forward. Getting this albatross off your neck may be some of the best money you spend. (Note to self: find place to donate albatross.)

Create Good Flow

Once you've gotten rid of all the extra stuff and organized the rest enough, the goal is to have a workable space with good flow. This then means maintenance. Make your organizational system quick, easy, and memorable so you're more likely to keep using it. Things should get put away based on how or when you would go looking for it. The putting away now is in the service of the retrieving next time. When your motivation is fading faster than the clutter, remind yourself of why you're putting in the effort. Think about how great it will feel to fly through your tasks without detours to look for something. Feel the satisfaction of having more time for whatever else is important to you. Feel the lack of dread when you walk into that space, knowing you can find that crucial item (didn't I see it over here somewhere?).

You don't have to love organizing and you don't need to be great at it. You just need to be good enough. Let go of the guilt and judgment and instead focus on how your life is better if you can continue to invest some energy in this.

Digital Clutter

Probably everyone struggles to keep up with email and generally to keep all those files, pictures, links, queues, etc. organized (enough). Cheap and essentially limitless storage allows us to keep everything—but can we find the right thing at the right time? Sometimes it feels like the only way to find the needle in the haystack is to set fire to all the hay.

Challenges with managing your digital life can have a big impact on your productivity—and also your reputation. So if this is one of your weak links, it's worth investing the energy to at least get somewhat more on top of it, even if it still feels like holding back the avalanche.

There's a lot that can be recommended when it comes to managing your digital life. As always, the easy part is rattling off the strategies—the hard part is using them every day, even when you're totally slammed. This little section won't solve all your problems, but here are some guiding principles.

- **Use consistent names for files**. This makes them easier to find and to quickly see what's what. For example, "Pres ADHD Productivity CHADD 25-06.ppt" tells me the topic, who it's for, and when I did it. This is really helpful when I need to do a similar presentation.

- **Reduce incoming email**. Unsubscribe from as much as you can so the important ones don't get lost in the slightly interesting ones. Alternatively, set up filters or create a second email address for less important stuff.

- **Quickly delete the emails you won't read**. Swipe them away without thinking too much about it. If it's kind of interesting but you probably won't get to it, then just delete it now. Or if you may need to find it later, then archive it so it's searchable.

- **Don't spend more time organizing your digital life than it will save you in the retrieving**. Tags and folders for email can be helpful, as can folders for files, but since so much can be searched relatively easily, think about how useful these will really be. If you rarely need to go looking for something, it isn't worth spending the time to diligently file it away. A minute of scrolling through search results may get you the email or file quicker.

If your inbox is ten miles long or your file storage is a mess, it can feel overwhelming to look at it, not to mention hopeless that you will ever get it under control. This makes it really easy to avoid dealing with it, but that just makes it worse. So, like in other situations in life, you need to go towards that discomfort and invest the time to get it under some sort of control—kind of. If your situation isn't that bad, it may be worth blocking out some time to plow through your inbox or file storage and deal with everything, get it organized, etc. If this feels like an achievable goal, then you're in pretty good shape. Most likely though, it feels impossible to catch up and you would rather eat your computer than spend that long in front of it. This brings us to plan B: Starting Over.

> Changing your identity in the witness protection program is not a viable method of managing your digital life.

There comes a point where it isn't worth spending tons of time to organize and deal with old stuff that's unlikely to be needed again. In this case, declare organizational bankruptcy and accept the idea that you will wipe the slate and start fresh today. For your files of various kinds, move all the old stuff into a folder called something like Old Stuff 2025. As you use those old files or create new ones, save them into your new organizational system and with the new naming system. The stuff you never go back to can just sit there, in case you ever need it. Don't waste time organizing things you will never use.

It's the same concept for your email. The problem with going through all of your old email is that the new ones keep coming so you never catch up. The only solution is to declare email bankruptcy and move all the old ones out of your inbox and into archives so you don't see them (and have a panic attack). For most people, once an email passes a certain age, it's unlikely to still be relevant. If it somehow comes up later, you can always search for it and read it then. Maybe take some time to think about whether there are specific older emails that you know you need to deal with and grab those, but otherwise decide where you're making the cut—one month? Two months? Then quickly deal with the rest until you get current. If you worry about missing something important, console yourself that it will likely pop back up when you get a reminder or angry email. That's not an ideal solution, but it's better than slogging through a million old emails—by which I mean never actually getting around to slogging through all those emails.

Once you've gotten your digital life generally up to date or close enough, then you're in the maintenance phase. This might feel less oppressive, but it still requires a regular input of time and mental energy, like it or not. I would even go so far as to say that if your inbox continues to expand, then *something* isn't working in your life. Maybe you're just avoiding email, but also maybe it reflects that you have too much on your plate, or you need to get better at saying no, or you're being too much of a perfectionist, or you're depressed, or something... It's a red flag. If your out-of-control inbox reflects something bigger, then invest the energy to address it and take care of yourself. If it simply reflects not giving your email the time that it seems to need, then bite the bullet and accept that living a good life requires you to spend enough time on email. It just does.

Put It to Work

- Identify what you do that contributes to your clutter and disorganization. Where does most of this stuff come from? Why does it stick around so long? What can you tell yourself to move things along a bit more?

- Pick one area and purge the stuff you don't really need, then put away the rest. How much stuff did you get rid of? How different does the space look? Notice how it's more efficient and less stressful to work in this space.

- Think about your digital life. How quickly can you find the files you need? How many emails do you have in your inbox? If your digital state of affairs is worse off than you would hope, what can you do today to make at least a small improvement?

- ## What, When, Where, and Why?

What strategies are you going to apply from this chapter? How will this be different from what you're already doing? Or perhaps have done before?

When and where? The more specific you can be, the better. Then actively look for these moments. Or set an alarm or other reminder to pull your attention to it. How can you set things up beforehand to make this easier to stick with?

Why? What problem will this solve or improve? What are all the direct and indirect benefits of this change? How is your life better for it? This is your motivation for when you don't feel like it.

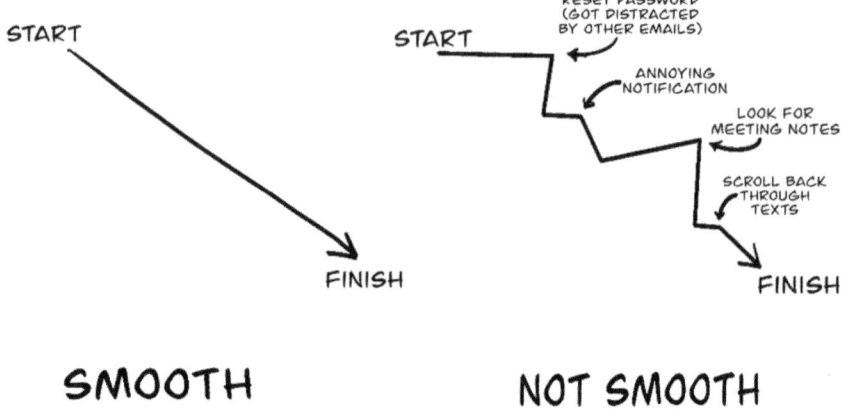

SMOOTH   NOT SMOOTH

18. Create a Smooth Workflow

I'M ALL ABOUT HELPING CLIENTS create processes that get things done well, predictably, and with the least amount of force of will. If you're already more likely to get distracted and derailed, then good processes are all the more important. Clunky processes create off-ramps because every bump, ping, friction point, and extra step is a chance to get off task. And then spend longer before getting back to it. For example, if you don't have a good password manager, then it's easy to get lost in your email while waiting for a password reset and maybe never get back to the original task. Or you go looking for the dishwasher tabs and wind up pulling everything out from under the sink to re-organize it.

The more these kinds of things happen, the more it undermines your faith in your ability to stay on track this time. If you do get off task, then all those other bad memories pile into this moment, which becomes yet another bad move to beat yourself up about. This self-doubt and self-flagellation become the psychological fallout of ADHD and only make it harder to create a future that is different from your past.

To counter this, it's worth the effort to streamline your processes and minimize the transitions. Invest the time to make your tasks easier to do. This will make it easier to talk yourself into starting whatever you need to do because it won't be as bad to do it. It will take less willpower to work your way through. And it will make it more likely that you will get all the way to the end, with all the right details, because— you'll be less likely to wander off task.

> Use your impatience for good by channeling it into efficient systems.

Think about what you do in an average week, whether it's the morning routine or some core feature of your job. If you do it often enough, even small improvements can add up. How can you make any of these tasks easier, faster, closer, simpler, more predictable, or fewer steps? It's too easy to take things as set, to not see options and alternatives, but change is possible.

Here's a personal example. In the old days, when I had new clients write out their information on paper (it's like a screen, but thinner), I would wind up with a stack that would eventually need to get filed, including reports I received, insurance paperwork, etc. When the stack got big enough, I would dutifully file it away alphabetically by last name. When my cabinet in the office got too full, I would pull out the clients I hadn't seen in a while and move them to my basement until I was legally allowed to shred them. In my defense, I would do the filing while I was on a conference call—the old-fashioned kind on the phone where no one could see my multitasking. After more years than I'm proud of, I realized that I almost never dug back into those files and that therefore there was no benefit from alphabetizing them. Duh. After that, I just filed them with the newest at the front. On the rare occasions that I needed to retrieve something, I could still find it pretty quickly. Not only did this realization save me some time, but it saved me my most boring time.

Look for those small opportunities. Good systems and strategies are usually created by persistently adding gradual refinements to OK ones. You don't need to make everything a well-oiled machine, but don't resign yourself to a pile of rusty, mismatched gears, either.

You might find yourself needing to balance efficiency and aesthetics, for example, when leaving some things out makes them easier to use but doesn't look great (mostly to your spouse). You may also find yourself needing to explain what works best for your efficiency to someone who prefers the more aesthetically pleasing option. Relationships need to take both people's preferences into account, but it might be helpful to explain why what is easy for them may not be easy for you (e.g., that what is out of sight is indeed out of mind). You may also want to explain how they stand to benefit from your greater efficiency. If they agree to do it your way, then show your gratitude by putting in the effort to do a good job of it.

The real goal here is to spend less time and mental energy on what you have to do so that you have more left for what you want to do, for what means the most to you. Not having time for what matters is the ultimate cost of losing bits of time in various places and getting knocked off track too often.

Don't be a perfectionist about this either. Sometimes you will take the long way around. But every time that you can stick to this smoother workflow is a little better than not. Just keep adding up those better times.

Put It to Work

- Identify a few of those small places that knock you off track. How long does it take to get back to where you started? How does that affect your productivity? Your feelings about yourself? How can you smooth over these bumps?

- Identify at least one pretty good workflow that you can refine to make even better. How would that make your day a little better?

- What can you tell yourself to make it more likely that you will keep using these better systems? How can you remind yourself of the benefits? How can you keep setting yourself up so that these better systems are easier to use?

- ## What, When, Where, and Why?

What strategies are you going to apply from this chapter? How will this be different from what you're already doing? Or perhaps have done before?

When and where? The more specific you can be, the better. Then actively look for these moments. Or set an alarm or other reminder to pull your attention to it. How can you set things up beforehand to make this easier to stick with?

Why? What problem will this solve or improve? What are all the direct and indirect benefits of this change? How is your life better for it? This is your motivation for when you don't feel like it.

SECTION V. SHARPEN YOUR TOOLS

WHO DOESN'T LOVE A FRESH, new notebook?

Someone with ADHD who has had it for a week, that's who. Maybe two weeks, if they're lucky.

This is the section where I will tell you what you have been told eight million times—you need a written schedule, to do list, and alarms/reminders. My goal is to say it in a way that's more helpful and less judgey. When you do it right, these become tools to build a better life for yourself, not just shackles that tie you to other people's demands.

Also, when you do it right, being seen using these tools can smooth over the social fallout when you do drop the ball occasionally since the other person is more likely to assume that you had good intent. You can get away with winging it if you hit the mark, but it's a bad look when you miss.

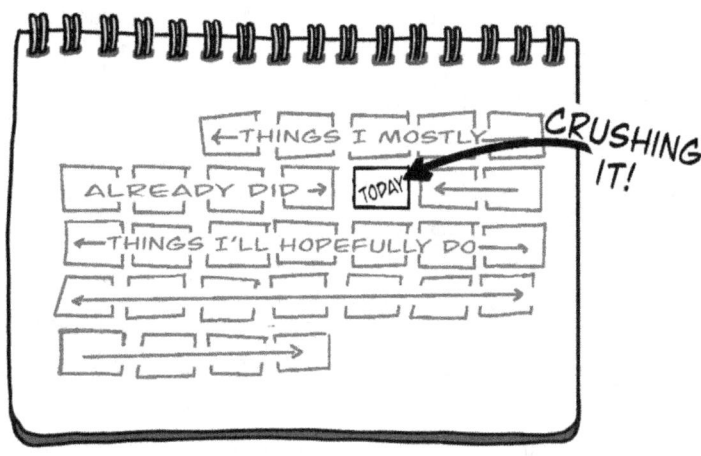

19. Yes, You Need a Real Schedule

IT'S HARD TO DO THE RIGHT thing at the right time if you don't know what you're supposed to be doing now. Therefore, schedules are for *what* and *when*. You might even go for bonus points by adding *how* and *where* the event will be happening and possibly with *who*. And if you're worried that you'll forget the reason for the event, you might even jot a note about *why*.

When a client tells me that they don't use a written schedule and just remember everything, almost never do I think to myself, "Wow, this person must have an amazing memory!" If I had any doubt on the question, the truth is usually revealed when these clients miss an appointment. Frankly, what is amazing is how well they sometimes do without a written schedule, but that can be part of the problem—they do just well enough to be able to (sort of) justify relying on memory. It's kind of like getting a D in a class—you still passed, technically.

If I ask these clients about it, they usually explain that they've tried various schedules in the past but had trouble sticking with them, so they gave up. I get it that it feels pointless, but sometimes the problem is that they're expecting too much from a humble schedule, whether it's old school paper, simple online calendar, or expensive app/platform/fad/cult.

> If you can remember everything you have going on in your life, then you don't have enough going on in your life.

The job of a written schedule is mostly to help with planning—e.g., I have that meeting at 2:00 on Tuesday. It might also help with awareness if you add an alarm for 1:45, thereby increasing the odds that you make that meeting. So far, so good. But what schedules don't do is create motivation—they don't make you do the prep work on Monday or make sure you show up on Tuesday. (See *6. What Exactly Is Getting in Your Way Here?* for more on the difference between planning, awareness, and motivation.) When clients tell me that schedules (or whatever tool) don't work for them, it's because they're expecting too much of them. Fortunately, there's partial credit to be had—if you scribble something in your schedule and then check it occasionally, you're more likely to do the right thing at the right time. It's a good start. The next section, *VI. Productivity is a Mental Game*, has tons of strategies on how to wrangle sufficient motivation. Or at least keep it from trickling away.

My first advice on schedules is to focus on creating a system that works well enough. I've seen clients get *really* into creating the perfect or prettiest schedule. I'm all in favor of creating a tool that works well and that you feel good using, but sometimes this can become its own procrastination if it takes the place of actually getting things done. After all, the folks at the meeting will be more impressed by your presence than by what shade of blue you used to indicate its relative importance. Honestly, if your schedule system was scribbling notes on your hand and it worked most of the time, I would tell you to keep it.

Once you have your good enough system, try to use it as often as you can. Even if you only use it half the time, that's still half better than never using it. Your life is tangibly better off for it. Get away from that all-or-nothing thinking that makes it easy to give up at the first sign of trouble. Even if you miss the 2:00 meeting, the folks at the 3:30 meeting will be happy you're there. Unfortunately, no one is happy about the 4:30 meeting...

The more you use your schedule, the better it works. Every time you look at it, whether to see what's coming or to add something, is a quick reminder. Since I see clients every hour and therefore schedule the next session at the end of every hour, I'm never surprised by anything in my schedule because I've seen it a hundred times before it happens. You probably don't live in your schedule this much, so you might need to ingrain the habit of checking your schedule from time to time, such as at the start, middle, and end of day. Setting an alarm or taping up a small reminder might help. Or every time you add something, make a point of looking to see what else is already on that day and also what's coming up later today. In *20. And Probably a To Do List, Too* I will talk more about putting tasks into your schedule, which will put them in front of your eyes more often. If you don't have a lot of scheduled events in your day, it's probably best to set some alarms to remind you about appointments because there will be bigger blocks of time where you're loose in the wild. These alarms will almost certainly be more reliable than just noticing the time.

I also recommend putting useful notes right into the schedule entry. For example, the address, phone number, confirmation number, what you need to bring, etc. Most likely you have all this right there when you're putting the appointment into your schedule. This saves a lot of last minute scrambling and running late. I have a client who felt really good about being a few minutes early for his doctor's appointment...until he realized he showed up at the wrong office. Dang it! That would have been good to include, and in all caps. This is one of those classic ADHD places where a small action or inaction causes big headaches later.

Do I Have To?

It's easy to have a love/hate relationship with your schedule. Or maybe vague fondness/hate. You probably recognize the benefit but also hate the stress of needing to make yourself do things when you don't feel like doing them. And then there are all the bad feelings that come from, yet again, dropping the ball when you forget to add something to your schedule, forget to check it, or forget where the hell it even is if it's paper. Undoubtedly, you've also had more than enough experiences of someone making a snide comment about putting something into your schedule, which seems to be more about making you feel like crap than about remembering the appointment. Plus all those experiences as a kid with parents and teachers giving you a hard time about your schedule. Yes, all of that sucks.

The point of using a written schedule now is that it's an aid to achieving *your* goals. It's about accomplishing what is important to you and being more of the kind of person that you want to be. It's about making your life less chaotic and having fewer dropped balls to feel guilty about. That all seems pretty important.

> Schedules can be a stress or a salvation, but they're just a tool.

It's easy to say that you forgot to add something to your schedule or to check it—we all have our moments, after all. But also, sometimes we kind of give ourselves a little bit of a pass. As in, we tell ourselves that we will enter it later, something that we probably wouldn't bet a lot of money on working out. Or we say that we will just remember. Again, don't take that bet. I have more on this in *23. The Lies We Tell Ourselves*, but first, ask yourself how you let yourself off the hook of using your schedule. How does that tend to work out? These are the moments for some blunt honesty, even if it means pushing ourselves to take that harder step.

Paper, Online, or Both?

For some people, a plain old paper schedule book is still the best way to go. It's quick and easy. I used one for years. The downside is that you won't always have it with you so you'll need to scribble a note or remember to add something later, which can be a real roll of the dice. And if your schedule goes missing, you're doomed to wander aimlessly while you attempt to reconstruct everything you committed to. Also, paper schedules can't beep at you to tell you that it's time to go.

Probably most of us use online schedules these days and for good reason. This is especially true if you don't have that many scheduled events—if most of the time that you check your schedule there isn't much on it, you're going to stop checking it. Obviously. Instead, be sure to set alarms to let you know that something is coming. This might be right before, but if something is first thing in the morning or requires prep, then you may want an alarm the day before as well. There's a bit of an art to setting an alarm at the right time.

Take advantage of different colors or tags for different types of events, but don't go crazy with it. Make it quick and easy to assign or you'll stop using them. Personally, I use three: client sessions, non-client meetings or presentations, and personal.

As much as possible, try to avoid keeping two schedules. This is a total set up for something getting entered or changed in one but not the other. Even so, you might have to use one for work and one for home because of security or privacy issues. If you can't sync them, then think of them more as your workday schedule and your personal time schedule. If you have a dentist appointment in the middle of the day, put that in your work schedule. If you have an evening work event that will interfere with family time, put it in your personal schedule, too. Put these rogue events in the place where you put other events that might conflict with it or where you will be looking when it's getting towards time to go.

If you have a romantic partner, synch your schedules or share events so you can avoid those really fun debates about whether you told them about something. Alternatively, create a written trail by sending an email or text as soon as something gets scheduled that may impact the other. This way the memory is captured externally rather than in our internal memory, which tends to fail us. Unless you need to jump away from a car speeding at you, force yourself to take those extra steps and not buy into the optimistic belief that you will enter it into your schedule later or remember to tell your partner.

In all of this, keep reminding yourself that your schedule is a tool that helps you do the job of knowing what to do when. Figure out the simplest method to do that job. Then keep doing it.

In case you need a cautionary tale for the risks of not using your schedule (which you don't), some of the time for editing this chapter was available when a client missed his appointment because he didn't put it into his schedule. As he wisely noted, "Admittedly, this is kind of on brand for me."

Put It to Work

- How well does your current schedule system work for you in terms of tracking what you need to? In terms of your stress level? What refinements would make it work better for you?

- Notice how you let yourself off the hook of checking or putting things into your schedule. How does that tend to work out in terms of what you manage to keep track of? Your stress level? Your relationships with others? How can you remind yourself of the benefits of using your schedule more?

- How often do the times for scheduled tasks slip by unnoticed? How much of a problem is it when they do? How helpful would it be to set alarms for some of your scheduled tasks? How can you remind yourself of this?

- ## What, When, Where, and Why?

What strategies are you going to apply from this chapter? How will this be different from what you're already doing? Or perhaps have done before?

When and where? The more specific you can be, the better. Then actively look for these moments. Or set an alarm or other reminder to pull your attention to it. How can you set things up beforehand to make this easier to stick with?

Why? What problem will this solve or improve? What are all the direct and indirect benefits of this change? How is your life better for it? This is your motivation for when you don't feel like it.

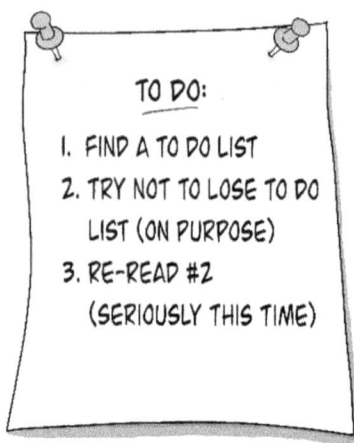

20. And Probably a To Do List, Too

LIFE HAS WAY TOO MANY loose ends. What's coming, what's going, what's the deal with this thing anyway? In the midst of this constant flow of ideas and demands, our internal memory never works as well as we hope it will. This leads to a lot of "Holy crap!" moments. Too stressful. And it tends to justify other people getting judgey or over-involved in your business. No thanks. The solution is to externalize this remembering by using something outside of our heads to keep track. We do this in all sorts of ways:

- Official paper list

- Web-based or app to do list

- Sticky notes

- Notebook

- Whiteboard

- Send yourself an email, text or voicemail

- Scribbled scrap of paper

- Leaving items out as their own reminder (e.g., empty dish detergent container, tab in your browser)

- Using a random item as a reminder (i.e., the old trick of tying a piece of string around your finger)

These are all good strategies. Whatever you can do to reduce the demands on your internal memory, the less stressful your life will be. If you find yourself too often forgetting to do things, then it's time to get serious about how you can capture those ideas and ensure they don't drift into the void before you check that box. Frankly, needing some sort of a to do list shouldn't be surprising. By the time you graduate middle school, your life has probably expanded to a point where it's almost impossible to "just remember" everything you need to do. Unless one of the things you need to remember is to wear a blue shirt for spirit day, you should probably read this chapter.

To Do Lists Don't Have to Suck

It's easy to hate your to do list, to feel like it just stresses you out. You may even feel like you're in an abusive relationship with your to do list. When life is overwhelming, it can feel like your ever-expanding to do list just rubs your face in it by spotlighting everything that you *still* haven't gotten to. It's tempting to change your name and hide from your to do list so you don't get the painful reminders.

Despair not! There is hope! Sort of!

I'm not going to suggest that all it takes to manage your ADHD is a good to do list, but I am also not going to blame all your troubles on its absence either. Lots of other things need to happen too (see every other page in this book), but a good enough to do list makes life much easier.

Most importantly, an effective to do list is an aid to living a better life—to living *your* better life. It's an ally, not a dictator. You may not love it, but you shouldn't hate it. When you feel a little queasy at the thought of your to do list, remind yourself of how it makes your life better. The list doesn't create obligations, it just records them, but it can be overwhelming to see it all at once. It's kind of like blaming the light that helps you see how much junk you have in your basement—it's really not about the light. An out of control to do list reflects other problems where tasks are being added faster than they are completed or ditched. If this is the case, then, again, see every other page in this book.

Put To Dos into Your Schedule

Diligently scribbling down to dos is a good start and definitely better than those times that you convince yourself that you'll just remember it. (No comment.) Unfortunately, just because something gets written down doesn't guarantee that the task will be completed. If only. This is the problem with to do lists—tasks can sit there forever. "Is *now* the time to work on that? Hmm. Maybe it's time to do that other thing instead—it's been there a while. Or that one..." We still need to invest the cognitive effort to sort through and decide what to do right now, then muster the motivation to actually do it.

The advice I give is to make tasks time-specific (and more likely to be completed) by putting them into your schedule. This converts it from just an idea, a possibility, to an actual intention. Or maybe even a plan. Planning makes it real. This could be something specific like comparing car insurance plans or something more general like working on marketing. Or maybe even set aside a block of time for Things I'm

> Writing something down is a good start. Giving it a specific time is even better.

Avoiding. Think of it as an appointment with yourself with an agenda and everything. Add in some snacks if that makes you more likely to show up and stay to the end. Rather than just reacting to whatever pops up or hoping that somehow this task will get done at some point, plan out at least some of your time. This is especially helpful if there are time constraints, like needing to make calls during business hours or really immerse yourself in a project while it's quiet. This is also helpful if you tend to take too much on because you forget how much you already have to do. If you drop a bunch of these tasks into your schedule, you might see that you don't really have time for whatever else just piqued your interest or was asked of you.

This intentional planning is especially important for those deep work projects—the ones where we really need to think a lot about them, hold a bunch of information in mind, work our way through a complicated process, make some hard choices, etc. Maybe you can fold laundry when you're half-dead, but these are the projects that demand your A game so there's no margin for error. Schedule this work for your best times and then be really intentional about conserving your energy/mood and showing up in a productive mindset. This might begin with getting a good night of sleep, possibly working out, bringing a snack, etc. Crank up some loud music and run around high-fiving people if that helps. This is important, so give it the effort it deserves.

A lot of folks are hesitant to commit like this because they worry it won't work out or that something else will get in the way. Fine. That task you added to your list is not a blood oath—just move it somewhere else. Preferably don't just delete it or skip over it—find another place to move it to. In general, things that are scheduled earlier in the day are more likely to be completed because they don't get knocked out by the day's unfolding events. If there's something that you really need to get done, take an extra couple seconds to think about where the best place is to put it in your schedule—what happens before, what needs to be done next, what else might be happening at that time, what your energy level will be, etc. We all tend to be optimists about how things will work out, so really think about all the random stuff that might pop up and ruin your great plan. Then think about how you will deflect those intrusions and stick to your plan.

At a more emotional level, there's also the hesitation that when Thursday afternoon arrives, for example, you just won't feel like scheduling ductwork cleaning. Besides the obvious point that of course you won't feel like it (why would you?), asking yourself whether you *want* to do it is the wrong question. The better question is, how can I motivate myself to do this anyway? As in, how do I remind myself of the benefits of doing this now by feeling the benefits or satisfaction I will have afterwards?

I'm not going to pretend that it's easy to make yourself do it in the moment. Fortunately, I have all of *Section VI. Productivity is a Mental Game*, to address all the ways that we make things complicated.

149

You can also use scheduling blocks of time for a task as a way to take advantage of your procrastination-driven hyperfocus. Sometimes tasks will expand to fill the time available, so if you know that you have a set amount of time, it may kick you into gear sooner and compress the work time. This may be especially helpful for those tasks that can kind of go on forever because there are always more tweaks you can do. By having a set amount of time, it may force you to get to good enough quickly, polish what you can, and then move on when you run out of time.

Clear the Dead Wood

To do lists are a helpful tool, but they can easily become graveyards of failed hopes, an official record of your shortcomings. (Yep, there's another thing I never got to...) This is where good intentions come to die.

OK, maybe. But an effective to do list is a living document that adapts and changes with the times. Tasks get added. Tasks are completed and crossed off. Priorities are re-shuffled. And some tasks get kicked off undone—don't call us, we'll call you.

The first place to improve your relationship with your to do list is to intentionally pause to consider whether a task even makes the cut of getting written down. As in, do you actually have time for this task? And if you do, is it important enough that you're actually going to get to it before it becomes irrelevant (e.g., I'm not two weeks late with my Thanksgiving decorations; I'm fifty weeks early). As a client wisely said, "Am I planning or just writing this down?" It can take some real cognitive effort to figure this out, but it's probably worth the upfront cost. If you want to do a deep dive on this,

> It's easy to be optimistic about the future despite being pessimistic about the past.

which is definitely not procrastinating on learning more fascinating lessons about to do lists, then check out *Section III. What Are You Working Towards?*

You probably also have tasks on your to do list that, in your defense, were pretty reasonable when you added them, but life has moved on and they're still not done. For good reasons or bad, they're no longer worth doing. Or they're only sort of worth doing—enough to make you hesitant to dump them, but not enough to give them your time. They're in that annoying grey zone that makes you feel slightly guilty every time you see them—and then keep seeing them because you never actually complete them. Besides the fact that it adds stress and bad feelings to your day to have a bunch of this so-so junk loitering on your to do list, it's also distracting in that more important tasks get lost in all the duds. It's tempting to tell ourselves that we should keep these so-so tasks just in case we have time (of course, if it hasn't happened yet...), but we ignore the cost that it brings.

Therefore, make your to do list survival of the fittest by only keeping the tasks that are still worthy. No loyalty to old ghosts. This means making an honest assessment of whether you're actually going to get to this or if it's wiser to cut it loose. Maybe the time for this task has passed, or maybe you're just not that into it (which might explain why it's still on your list). You may feel guilty while you delete these tasks, but you will probably feel relieved after. Frankly, if you complete every single thing on your to do list, then you probably need to dream bigger. There are always more ideas than time, so remind yourself that completing the worthiest gives you the freedom to dump whatever didn't make the cut. Really successful people are great editors—they know when to let go the tasks, projects, and goals that no longer add enough value so they can pour all their energy into what adds the most.

Tolerate the Feelings that Arise

Of course, deleting unfinished tasks from your to do list is very reasonable and all, but it can get more complicated when those hanging commitments bring guilt and shame. They can feel like a testament to your inability to get things done, proof of your being less than. Every line reminds you of every other dropped ball that you feel bad about, which makes for a much stronger visceral response than any one task deserves. This makes it really easy to avoid your to do list entirely and, ironically, also harder to cross off these items and move on. As much as all those unchecked lines are a painful reminder, it can feel like they aren't yet a failure if you keep them on your list (someday...). There's that stubborn hope of salvation, that somehow the time will appear where you can complete this task and shed the shame and guilt. All of this is way too big a burden to bear—and far more than an unfinished task deserves.

This is yet another one of those places where some acceptance and self-compassion can set you free. Even if you really did totally blow it on a task that you could have completed but didn't, that doesn't obligate you to suffer for the rest of your life. Look that disappointment square in the eye. Acknowledge how you feel about it—all of the feelings, including guilt, shame, sadness, hopelessness, frustration, even anger. Recognize that you would do it differently if you could do it again—or at least try to. Accept that holding onto this obligation now doesn't change the past—nor does punishing yourself with it. Accept that life has probably moved on and this task may not be as relevant as it once was. Recognize that there were other things happening at the time that took your attention. Remind yourself that you have the right to make choices about what you do and don't do, and that life always has more tasks than time. Remind yourself that beating yourself up for old tasks makes you less effective at dealing with new tasks. The goal here isn't to get rid of any uncomfortable feelings, but to tolerate them and reduce the extent to which they hold you hostage by overly influencing what you do next.

> Writing something down on a to do list does not make it a moral obligation.

It can be helpful sometimes to use some sort of ritual to let things go. Maybe you write all these never-to-be-finished tasks onto a separate list called Letting It Go. Or Good Riddance. Or even, Leave Me the Hell Alone. Maybe you speak some words honoring the hope you felt when you wrote them down, acknowledging the disappointment that they were never completed and affirming that it is time for your life to move on without them. Do it as a break-up where you drop the list into recycling and walk away. Or do it as a funeral where you bury it. Hell, do it as a Viking funeral where you build a little boat, set the list off to sea, and shoot a flaming arrow into it. Maybe invite some friends if that will help—hugs all around.

If you have some tasks that you really want to get to and you aren't tortured by them, then create a second aspirational list. This isn't your main to do list that you work off of, but rather it's the place to keep all those tasks that you hope to get to one day. Knock yourself out on this one. Make this one as long as you want; just be sure that your main to do list doesn't require you to live to two hundred.

Put It to Work

- Think about your existing to do lists and reminders—how well do they work for you? When do things fall through the cracks? How big a problem is that? What would improve your to do lists? How could you encourage yourself to use them more often?

- Identify some tasks on your to do list to add to your schedule. When would be the best times to do them? How might they be affected by what precedes them? Notice how this helps you get them done.

- Find some items on your to do list that have been there for a while and dump them off. How much less stressful is it to look at your to do list? Do the other items on your to do list stand out more with less clutter around them?

- ## What, When, Where, and Why?

What strategies are you going to apply from this chapter? How will this be different from what you're already doing? Or perhaps have done before?

When and where? The more specific you can be, the better. Then actively look for these moments. Or set an alarm or other reminder to pull your attention to it. How can you set things up beforehand to make this easier to stick with?

Why? What problem will this solve or improve? What are all the direct and indirect benefits of this change? How is your life better for it? This is your motivation for when you don't feel like it.

IN THE GRAND ARC OF HUMAN HISTORY, WHAT DOES *"NOW"* EVEN MEAN, REALLY?

21. Wait, What Was I Supposed to Be Doing Now?

USUALLY WHEN WE TALK ABOUT memory, we talk about remembering the past, but there is also a part of our memory that involves remembering into the future (e.g., "ooh, I need to call her tomorrow"). This is our *prospective memory,* which carries plans from the present into the future. It's our mental to do list. It might be two seconds from now or a year or more.

Prospective memory glitches can add a lot of stress, as can the effort of repeatedly reminding ourselves of what we need to do (and worry that we will still forget). We're more likely to forget to do something when we're really absorbed in another task, especially if it's different from what we're trying to remember, such as working from home makes it harder to remember to ask a coworker something. Interruptions can also wipe the slate clean in a flash as our attention shifts from remembering to whatever just happened.

How well our prospective memory works has big social ramifications. It's not just that it carries plans into the future—it carries *intentions*. If you forget to do something, it's easy for others to assume that it wasn't important enough to you to be worth remembering, that you didn't really intend to do it. Until someone creates an app that can read people's thoughts, we look at others' actions to infer their intentions. I say that ADHD is a disorder of reliably

> ADHD is all about *performance*. Therefore, solutions are all about the *point of performance*.

converting intentions into actions, which means you will have more experiences where what you say you intend to do doesn't match up with what you wind up doing. If this happens too often, then others will look at your actions to infer not only your intentions, but also your character. Yikes...

Because ADHD is all about doing the right thing in the right moment, a lot of strategies focus on that crucial moment—the time, place, and/or situation—and how we can trigger that desired action. For example, putting the umbrella in front of the door so you grab it on the way out. Or leaving a voicemail on your work phone so you get it when you're at your desk. Or setting an alarm. The less distance or time between the reminder and the action, the more likely you are to act on it. Even so, we've all had humbling experiences where we manage to forget in the blink of a moment. The goal is to improve your overall batting average.

Let Reminders Remember

We all love to think that we will remember, especially when we don't feel like making a note or setting an alarm. Unfortunately, life tends to have a way of disproving that optimism, especially if you have ADHD. Fortunately, there are ways of upping your batting average.

One is to not wait for the future and do the task now. Mission accomplished, no memory required.

The other way is to accept the frailty of the human condition and just create a goddamn reminder. Any way that holds that idea until you're able to act on it is probably more reliable than using internal memory. After all, tying some string around your finger is rarely a reminder to buy more string, so anything that will jar your attention will shake loose the memory. Then don't get rid of the reminder until you've actually completed the task— all the way to the end. (You probably don't need me to explain that last part.)

> Many memory problems are actually attention problems.

Schedules help us remember what to do when. To do lists are also prospective memory aids but aren't necessarily tied to a particular time, place or event—the reminder just sits there until we look at it and decide to act on it. So they're more general than specific, more passive than active.

Probably more effective are the reminders that get triggered at a particular location or event. Sticky notes placed in the relevant location, like on the inside of the front door, work better since they're closer to where the action is. Same for when we use an item as its own reminder, like when we put our lunch bag next to the coffee maker to remind us to grab our lunch from the fridge. We can also get fancier with location-based alarms on our phone where it will pop up a reminder when we are in a particular location. This could be something like reminding us to buy light bulbs whenever we happen to be in the hardware store, but it could also be something sooner like reminding us to mail something when we arrive at work. Or reminding us to call home every time we get to a particular point in our commute.

Then there are the standard time-based reminders which could be setting an alarm for Wednesday at 3:00 or a countdown timer for twenty minutes. Or attaching an alarm to a calendar event, like ten minutes before your meeting. If noticing time isn't your superpower, you would probably benefit from sprinkling alarms liberally into your day. It sucks to put in all this hard work and then blow it at the last minute when the right time slips by unnoticed.

Reminders tend to work better when there isn't too much competition for your attention. If you're running around with your hair on fire or there are a million things going on, that reminder is unlikely to grab you and then stick in prospective memory. Anything else you can do to quiet the distractions and competition, the more likely the reminder will get the job done. So part of remembering well isn't actually about memory at all.

You may also need to think about when the reminder will go off and if you will be in a position to act on it—getting a notification in the car about something to do at home is unlikely to work out. The timing of the alarm really comes down to the specific moment when you will need to do something about the task, because having it pop up at some random point in your day won't be helpful. If you have something first thing in the morning or that will otherwise disrupt your morning routine, it's probably helpful to set a reminder the afternoon or evening before since an alarm right before the event might be too late—something many of my clients have discovered when I call them at 8:05 AM.

There's also the option of asking someone else for a reminder. If they're better at remembering or if they're doing something that makes the remembering easier (such as walking by your desk on the way to that meeting), then that seems like a good plan. You just need to be careful that the other person doesn't feel like they're working harder on your remembering than you are. Or that, in other ways, the relationship feels unbalanced to them. I've seen this go both ways. Some clients don't realize that they take more than they give and therefore ask for too much. But I've also had clients who are so worried about taking too much that they don't ask for enough. For example, by not wanting to ask for a reminder but then forgetting to do the task, which is even worse for the other person.

If you're going to ask for a reminder, it will go over much better if you first show the other person that you're putting in your own effort on remembering and will put in good effort on the doing after they remind you. For example, showing them that you're acting on the reminder rather than going back to what you were doing (with a likely outcome that is predictable to all). Extra points if the reminder is worth the effort because the other person also stands to benefit from you doing the task. It's not their job to be your executive assistant, but having some skin in the game does make it easier to be generous. Again, you still need to show that you're putting in your own effort.

Optimize Your Mental Game

We can't set a reminder for every single thing we do (e.g., put milk back in fridge). As much as I'm a fan of good tools and systems, sometimes we need to rely on our internal abilities. This could be as we navigate the flow of events through our day or when we think of something to do but aren't really in a position to capture it. Fine. We can still make it more likely that everything will go according to plan.

We're all less likely to remember to do something when we're absorbed in an engaging or demanding task. There isn't that little bit of background attention to pop up the memory until we hit a break and suddenly remember—and panic.

> How often you wish for a time machine to go back to the past is a good indicator of how well you remember the future.

Therefore, one bit of advice is to avoid really engaging activities before you need to transition to something else. If it's interesting enough that you tend to lose track of time, then it's going to be a real roll of the dice as to whether you lift your head up at the right time. It's better to do something less enthralling or, alternatively, to get right to it—for example, driving to the appointment early and then doing stuff on your phone. It still doesn't guarantee that you will walk in the door on time even if you're in the parking lot half an hour early, but hopefully the odds are better.

It's also helpful if we have small moments of pause in our days. Breaks in the action where we can let our minds go into neutral, where we're not actively in gear. As our mind wanders around, those random thoughts have space to pop up. This is why showers can foster such great ideas and help with remembering. Or waiting for an elevator. Or watching the coffee brew. It's tempting to fill every single one of these moments with our phones, but sometimes it's helpful to just sit in that mental space and see where our minds go. The default for most of us is to fill every silence, to avoid just sitting with our thoughts. I know, it's boring, but sometimes something great shows up if we can leave the space open for a few minutes.

You may even want to take occasional moments through your day to mentally sort through what's going on to see if you suddenly remember a loose end. Probably the best times to do this are during existing transitions from one activity to the next. Make a point sometimes to pause for a beat or two before jumping into the next task or grabbing your phone to fill the space. Even fifteen seconds may be enough to pop up an idea or two. This obviously requires that your day isn't too much of a scramble, of rushing straight from one thing to the next, because that makes it easy to forget things—and set up tomorrow's scramble. This is where everything else in the book comes in...

Visualize Remembering

Sometimes we think of something that we need to do later but can't create a reminder. Maybe you're driving or with someone where you can't pull out your phone. Or lying in bed. Damnit, now what? One memory trick is to think about where and when you will want to remember—such as when you see your coworker tomorrow and can talk to them. Think about something in that situation that can serve as a reminder, as in, if they mention something about your joint project. Or just generally think about what they look like and how you might greet each other. Burn that image and dialogue into your memory so the recognition tickles your memory when it happens. This is your trigger, the situation that your brain recognizes and realizes there's something special about it. You want that little tingle in the back of your mind to prompt you to think more about it.

Think of it as the mental version of the old trick of tying a piece of string around your finger. For example, focus on something like your colleague's glasses—when you see them, you give yourself a little poke. Then visualize yourself saying, "Wait a sec! I need to ask you something!" Then reinforce it by burning the memory in a little more every time you think about it until you finally see that colleague. This strategy won't always work, but it is really nice when it does.

Put It to Work

- How can you show someone else that you had good intentions even when you forgot to do something? What can you tell them? Do you need to somehow make it up to them?

- How can you set yourself up in the point of performance (the time and place to act) to improve your prospective memory in the situations that you most commonly need to remember something? What can you set up—where, when, and how? What can you tell yourself in that moment to nudge yourself to set things up beforehand?

- Think about where you can add pauses in your day to reflect on your schedule and give those prospective memories a space to pop into. What are the natural transition points or quiet times in your day? Would it help to tape up a reminder or put these into your schedule?

- ## What, When, Where, and Why?

What strategies are you going to apply from this chapter? How will this be different from what you're already doing? Or perhaps have done before?

When and where? The more specific you can be, the better. Then actively look for these moments. Or set an alarm or other reminder to pull your attention to it. How can you set things up beforehand to make this easier to stick with?

Why? What problem will this solve or improve? What are all the direct and indirect benefits of this change? How is your life better for it? This is your motivation for when you don't feel like it.

22. You Get (Social) Points for Using Your Tools

PEOPLE HOPE FOR GOOD PERFORMANCE but will often settle for good intentions.

Think about that for a second. Yes, obviously it's important to do a good job when you can, but it's not just about what you manage to pull off. It's also about showing that you take your obligations seriously and that you're putting in the effort. Part of what this means is showing that you're working harder at managing your stuff than others are. I say that free passes are earned—others will be more forgiving when you run late, for example, if generally you show that you're working at it.

Using good tools and systems shows those good intentions. If someone sees you put the meeting into your schedule or if you confirm beforehand, they may give you some benefit of the doubt that something interfered with your good plan. If they don't see you record the meeting time, even if you do it later, it's easy for them to assume that that was the point of failure, that you didn't care enough to write it down. That may not be what actually happened, but their opinion of you will be based on what they see and how they interpret your actions.

Don't be a politician faking a photo op, but do make it easy for people to see that you're trying. I've had clients talk about feeling self-conscious about this, fearing that it shows how forgetful or whatever they are. I get it, but it's way better to be thought of as that person who always writes things down than that person who often forgets things. No contest. If they even notice it, the other person will see it as a sign of diligence and respect.

> ADHD makes it harder to follow through on your intentions, so make a point of showing them clearly.

If you're worried about how it will come across, then just give a quick explanation in a totally calm and natural way. Don't over-explain it or apologize because your insecurity will make people uncomfortable. Just say it straight: "Give me a sec to write that down, this is important." If you want to go for bonus points, maybe add something about how it benefits them—"I want to make sure I get you what you need." Nailed it.

I'm going to keep repeating this idea that the obvious part of managing ADHD is reducing the impact it has on your life, but that the equally important, less obvious part is to reduce the impact of whatever remains on how you interact with others and how you feel about yourself. Perfection not required.

Put It to Work

- Think about whether people believe you have good intentions when you drop the ball. If not, how can you make your intentions more clear by your actions? How can you explain what happened when you don't do what they're expecting?

- How can you make it more obvious that you're using your tools? How can you show that any slips are not for lack of effort (and thereby intentions)?

- Think up some quick and easy ways to explain the strategies that you're using and why they're helpful so you can whip them out when you need to. Practice saying them out loud so you feel comfortable using them.

- ## What, When, Where, and Why?

What strategies are you going to apply from this chapter? How will this be different from what you're already doing? Or perhaps have done before?

When and where? The more specific you can be, the better. Then actively look for these moments. Or set an alarm or other reminder to pull your attention to it. How can you set things up beforehand to make this easier to stick with?

Why? What problem will this solve or improve? What are all the direct and indirect benefits of this change? How is your life better for it? This is your motivation for when you don't feel like it.

SECTION VI. PRODUCTIVITY IS A MENTAL GAME

S INCE I'M A PSYCHOLOGIST, it shouldn't be surprising that this is the longest section. There's a good reason why I have so much content here: we do all sorts of weird, unhelpful, misguided, and kind of dumb things that shoot us in the foot. If people were perfectly rational, the world would be a very different place. I would spend my days swinging a hammer, junk food wouldn't exist, politics would be less frustrating, advertisers would assume we're smarter, and social media would be less maddening. Eight short chapters won't put a dent in all of that, but hopefully they will help you make some better productivity choices.

The overarching theme of this section is that you have more power than you think you do. You might give it away in various ways, often without knowing it, so the more aware you are of how you do this, the more you can hold onto your agency. The world is distracting and confusing and can easily knock down our good intentions, but you have the ability to keep your eye on the prize and bring your best to whatever life throws in your way.

ADHD is a neurologically based condition that can have a big effect on the types of experiences you have which can then have a big effect on how you see yourself. In other words, the neurological definitely shapes the psychological, especially before you understand how your struggles with forgetfulness, procrastination, misplacing things, etc. is neurologically-based. An accurate diagnosis and some targeted treatments and strategies can make a big difference in the experiences you have. A wise, ADHD-informed approach will put you much more on top of the demands in your life. It will still be hard sometimes to get things done, but a resilient mindset will keep you chugging along.

It's easy to blow it a couple times and then assume that nothing is going to change anyway, so why bother. If you had a bunch of years and a million experiences of seemingly good strategies not working, it's not unreasonable to get discouraged easily now. As much as catastrophizing gets a bad rap, it does serve the purpose of protecting us from disappointment, something you may feel you already have way too much experience with. Unfortunately, over-reading what a handful of experiences means and then throwing in the towel ignores what is different now and therefore why some optimism might be warranted.

So, I'll be honest: I'm asking you to take a risk here. This might not work out, and you may be disappointed again. Actually, I can guarantee that you will be disappointed, at least sometimes. My hope is that you have enough positive experiences to counterbalance those disappointments and that you can remind yourself that progress is rarely a straight line. Some setbacks will happen. Remind yourself of your successes. Tell yourself what you would tell your friend if they were down about it. Look at it as a learning opportunity to figure out what didn't work out. Focus on the next thing you can do, then do it well.

The chapters in this section are all about what happens in our heads, about how we think and feel about life's demands. A resilient mindset finds ways out of those mental dead ends, celebrates the victories, tolerates the failures, learns the right lessons, and grabs onto reasons to keep showing up.

23. The Lies We Tell Ourselves

LIFE IS HARD. SOMETIMES WE don't want to do that boring, uncomfortable, responsible thing when there's something much easier and more fun to do instead. This is why french fries exist. To make matters worse, we still want to see ourselves as saints while we enjoy the sin. We want it both ways. This is why diet soda exists. This is why Miller Lite claimed that it both tastes great and is also less filling, when clearly only one of those is true.

This is a universal struggle, that we want to see ourselves in a positive light even when we knowingly give in to temptation or take the shortcut. In order to pull this off, we find ways to justify these less than optimal decisions (e.g., by downsizing to the second largest order of fries). We use semi-plausible reasons to feel better about what we know isn't the best decision. For example, taking a break from working on a grueling report to check email—you know, in case anything important came in.

> Making the most of the present and making the most of the future are in a constant tug of war.

Life is full of tempting moments when willpower wavers. One of the ways of thinking about this is as a tug of war between doing what will make the present moment more enjoyable versus what will make a future moment better. For example, chatting with a coworker versus working on that big report that's due in a few days. If you have ADHD, you will feel more of a pull from the present and need to exert more effort to resist it in order to improve the future. (Go back to *3. ADHD Makes It Harder to Feel the Future* for more on this.) This can have massive effects on your productivity since getting things done mostly involves sacrificing in the present in order to create a better future.

I say that bad situations make bad choices more likely. The more stressful and chaotic your life is and the more depleted you feel, then the harder it is to muster the willpower to resist temptation and do that more responsible thing. It's too easy a fight for the present to win out over the future. This is where our favorite justifications come to the rescue—not by changing what we do, but by changing how we feel about what we're going to do anyway. It's impressive sometimes what we can talk ourselves into. We get to be a scoundrel with a heart of gold. If it makes you feel any better about what we can wind up believing, there was a time when doctors recommended smoking for its health benefits.

It's helpful to notice these little lies that we tell ourselves, these talking points that justify our less than optimal behavior. It's not my place to decide what you should do—the real arbiter is how you will feel about it after. If you're OK with how things worked out, great. It's when you will likely regret it later that maybe you should take a harder look at how you're trying to sell yourself on some awesome idea.

ADHD Makes Some Lies More Tempting

We all have some favorite lies based on the situations we find or place ourselves in and what we have the hardest time resisting. For example, someone who drinks too much will tell themselves that they really aren't drinking that much or that it isn't impacting their relationships. Someone with social anxiety will tell themselves that they don't really have much in common with the people at that upcoming gathering, so there's no point in going.

If you have ADHD, certain lies are more likely, such as:

- I don't have to write that down—I'll remember it
- This will only take a minute
- I will be more productive after I...
- I have plenty of time to work on that
- That task won't take that long
- I'll remember that I put this here
- I can do that tomorrow
- I don't have to go to bed now
- I'll put that away later
- I don't have to start getting ready yet
- I'll just watch one video

Any of these call out to you?

The problem with these lies is that sometimes they work. You know, except for all those times when they don't. It's tempting to feel lucky, as if this is one of those times when it will work out. All the benefit, none of the suffering! If we were really honest, we might be less optimistic about it working out well, but we like the idea that it will, so we run with it.

> Feeling lucky and being lucky are sadly not the same thing.

One of the ways to spot when you're trying to talk yourself into something dubious is that you use "just" to downplay it—e.g., "I'll just watch one quick video." That word is almost always a red flag since it's a handy way to round something down a little. By the way, you may also want to notice when your kids use that word with you. (Sorry, guys.)

> Beware of the slippery *just*.

It's also noteworthy that all of those lies involve ways to get out of doing the harder thing now that will benefit you later. They make the present moment more enjoyable or at least less unenjoyable. They kick the can down the road. This makes sense because of the way ADHD makes future consequences feel smaller. I have more on this in *3. ADHD Makes It Harder to Feel the Future,* which will explain a lot more than just why you sometimes talk yourself into bad ideas.

Be Honest About the Odds

My goal here isn't to be a buzzkill, but to make you more aware of where you get yourself into trouble. The good thing about identifying your favorite lies is that there are probably only a handful that cause the most heartache. That makes it much easier to keep an eye out for them.

The most important thing is to be honest with yourself about what you're doing and what the likely cost is. This way you're less likely to regret your decision later. No one needs more ill-fated decisions to beat themselves up over. The example I often use is that if I go to a concert, I accept that I will be more tired the next day, but it's worth it, so I feel good about that decision. This is different from watching one more episode of some show I can watch later and telling myself that I'll feel fine tomorrow—I know that's bogus and the fun isn't worth it the next day, so I will regret that choice.

Tolerate the Discomfort

These lies that we tell ourselves make an uncomfortable situation a little easier. They probably work in the moment, but then bring more discomfort later—it turns out that the universe and its consequences don't really care what we convince ourselves of.

The first step in being more honest with yourself is to reduce the number of situations where honesty is just too hard. The more stressful and chaotic your life is, the more willpower it takes to plow through—until you start to run low and the more shortsighted decisions seem more tempting. This is when those little lies begin to slip through. Getting more sleep, using your schedule more, and everything else in the book will probably be helpful here. Not that any of that is easy, but it's yet another reason to put in the effort to get your life under better control. And yet another reward for getting on top of your ADHD a bit more.

We all have our moments where we're tempted to believe our own sweet-talking. This is the moment of truth when we need to notice that we're lying to ourselves or at least shading the truth a bit. Maybe rounding things up or down to make them seem like a more reasonable option, like telling ourselves that one video is only twenty minutes (actually it's more than that) but also there's a strong possibility that we will watch more than one. The most important moment is that small space between having that tempting thought and acting on it. With ADHD, that space can be smaller and therefore make it harder to resist temptation. The goal in that moment is to pause just a moment longer so your conscious brain has time to kick in and remind yourself that this may not be the best idea. Seize that moment. Take a deep breath to stop yourself from whatever you're going to do next.

When you catch yourself using one of your favorite lies, here's the real test: If you had to throw down a fat stack of twenties and bet a thousand bucks of cold, hard cash, would you bet for or against this optimism? Picture that pile of bills and imagine everything you could do with it. Feel how much it would hurt to watch someone else pocket it. How do you feel about your odds now? Are you feeling a thousand bucks confident?

The chapters in the rest of this section deal with all the mental ways that productivity gets tangled up, such as perfectionism, overwhelm, ambiguity, etc. These are also uncomfortable and can make it tempting to lie to ourselves, so check out the upcoming chapters to make honesty easier.

Living with integrity and feeling good about yourself don't mean that you need to live like a monk. Hardly. It just means being honest about what you're doing and what the likely consequences are. As long as you are, you will feel good about yourself. As I've said before, the goal isn't to make you into a relentless productivity robot but to find the right balance between getting things done and enjoying a good life.

Put It to Work

- What are your three favorite lies? What do they (hopefully) allow you to get away with? What discomfort do they reduce? How do you feel, knowing that you're not being fully honest with yourself, even if it works out? How do you feel when it doesn't work out?

- What are the situations where you're most likely to lie to yourself? What is difficult or uncomfortable about those situations? How can you set yourself up beforehand to make the temptation to lie easier to resist?

- When you use your favorite lies, how often do they work out? How can you remind yourself of the cost if the lie doesn't work out? How can you really feel the benefit of doing the task in the present that will benefit your future?

- ## What, When, Where, and Why?

What strategies are you going to apply from this chapter? How will this be different from what you're already doing? Or perhaps have done before?

When and where? The more specific you can be, the better. Then actively look for these moments. Or set an alarm or other reminder to pull your attention to it. How can you set things up beforehand to make this easier to stick with?

Why? What problem will this solve or improve? What are all the direct and indirect benefits of this change? How is your life better for it? This is your motivation for when you don't feel like it.

24. Just Bite the Bullet on Things You Hate

IT'S TEMPTING TO CONVENIENTLY AVOID what we don't want to do—life has plenty of obligations that fit into this category. They're usually labelled as "the responsible thing to do" by the self-righteous, which really only makes them even less desirable to do. Pass... If you have ADHD, then what may just be boring for someone else may feel painful and exhausting to you. And, obviously, you'll feel as if it took ten times longer than the clock somehow indicates. (Maybe the battery is dying?)

Tempting as it is to pretend that you didn't get the memo, life has a way of dishing out consequences for not getting around to certain tasks. Best case, it's just as bad to do it later as it is to do it now. More likely though is that it somehow gets worse with time. For example, you miss out on doing something better when you're finally forced to deal with whatever you've been avoiding, or it's late and you're dragging. You may also lose options by waiting, like when reservations get all booked up. Or you need to buy the more expensive option that's the only thing in stock when you do get around to pulling the trigger. The ADHD tax strikes again.

Even if somehow you're lucky enough to dodge any consequences, at least this time, at least so far, there are still the psychological costs. First, there's the worry that you will eventually have to pay the piper, that someone will suddenly call you out. Busted. Second, even if you somehow make it to the end of class without revealing that you didn't do the reading, so to speak, you still know you didn't do it. While you may try to spin it as you're blessed with good luck and a brilliant ability to look confidently knowledgeable, all this faking it can wear on your image of yourself. If you really struggle with this kind of self-doubt, check out *31. Social Pressure, Faking It, and Falling Short.*

Having a conscience is a real bummer sometimes, so it's worth it to find ways to bite the bullet when you need to. Some tasks run on a regular schedule, such as paying bills or filling out weekly reports. For these, you may find it best to drop them into your schedule on repeat. Perhaps in red pen or something. Even if it's a one-time task, you may still find it helpful to plan where and when you will tackle it. Or maybe just have a regular time where you plow through whatever tasks you're avoiding. I talk more about putting to do list tasks into your schedule in *20. And Probably a To Do List, Too,* so be sure to add reading that to your to do list.

> Don't forget to give yourself extra credit for the tasks that are the hardest to make yourself do.

The rest of the book has plenty of other ways to make things easier or at least less hard. So look for all the ways that you can smooth down the frustrating parts, make boring tasks go a little faster, feel less anxious, etc. The less awful a task is, the less motivation it will take to get it done. This not only makes it more likely to happen, it also preserves more of your precious motivation for other stuff.

Get That Ball Rolling

I would love to guarantee that there are ways to make it fun or easy to do the things that you hate, but I'm not stupid enough to think that you're stupid enough to believe it. Here's what I can guarantee: you will still kind of hate it. Not very inspiring, but honest. The goal is to hate it less.

One way to hate it less is to tackle undesirable tasks when you've got more mental gas in the tank rather than waiting until you're running on empty but have to do it anyway—slogging through mental mud is a good way to hate it more. So, bite the bullet when you're well rested, have good focus, your meds are working, you just worked out, you had a snack, etc.—whatever brings more of your A game. That way you can plow through quickly and move on to better things.

Related to this, I often recommend scheduling your avoided tasks for earlier in the day since it's less likely they will get squeezed out by the day's events (even though you're hoping that they will).

You may also want to add in some small reward to top off your motivation. For example, after you finish a task or do a certain amount of work, you let yourself do something more enjoyable. This is a nice idea in theory but it's hard to stick to it, so your reward shouldn't be too tempting or you'll skip over the work. Also, if you're hoping to get back to work, you may also want to avoid rewards that tend to keep you stuck, like algorithm-driven online content. Or beer. (OK, so that's a weak joke, but I have had some college students who had to learn that lesson the hard way. Repeatedly.)

You can also set up some accountability by telling someone else what you're going to work on. Even if you just mention it in passing, that may be enough to make the difference. To really turn up the heat, tell them you will let them know when you're done. You might ask them to check in later if they're OK with that, but you don't want to create a situation where too much of the initiative is coming from someone else. If you do recruit someone else, you may want to coach them on what to say or how to say it (and also how not to say it), so they don't inadvertently do more harm than good. No one needs more nagging or judgment even if it is well-intentioned.

Accountability partners are pretty standard advice and they can be helpful, but I think it's important to be clear on how they work, especially if you have a bit of an oppositional streak. Unless this other person actually moves your body to do the task, it's still you choosing to do it. They don't make you do anything. Rather, their presence makes you face your own feelings about not holding to your commitment since there's someone there to witness you wiggling out. It's harder to ignore, minimize, or gloss over feeling guilty or disappointed under the accountability partner's cold and knowing stare. If you're the one who does the task, then you still get credit for it. And for being smart enough to set up a winning strategy.

You could also make it more entertaining by adding a ridiculous bet—as in, some ridiculous thing that you don't really want to lose but won't cost you any fingers. This could be something like you have to eat whatever appetizer of their choice or you have to pretend to love an episode of a show that kind of makes you nuts. Or explain to them why your favorite team's biggest rival has a lot going for them this season. Or sing the song of their choice, complete with dance moves. Good times. It adds a fun competitiveness to it all and is fun for both people, regardless of who wins or loses.

It's also important, when you do knock off that dreaded task, to take a moment to give yourself credit for it. You might push back on this idea by saying that you shouldn't give yourself credit for doing what you should do anyway. I push back on *that* by pointing out that you would almost certainly knock on yourself for, yet again, not doing it. So, fair's fair. If you had a bunch of years of undiagnosed and untreated ADHD, you have had more than enough experiences of knocking on yourself. Let's start evening that score.

We Knowingly Set Up Failure

Sometimes when we don't want to do something, we preemptively wiggle out of it by not putting it onto our to do list or schedule or setting an alarm. Whoops! Then, shockingly, we forget to do it. Is this motivated forgetfulness? Intentionally unintentional? A way to dodge the bullet without admitting that we decided not to do it? This might look like a time management or memory problem, but it's actually more about motivation and commitment—or lack thereof. Ideally, it would probably be better to make a real decision beforehand. You may decide that you're not doing it, at least not yet, and be OK with letting it go. This is probably how the story ends anyway. But chances are good that you will feel better about yourself if you didn't do it because you actively decided not to than you would if you just plain didn't get it done.

Alternatively, you may decide that, unfortunately, you really should just do the task. In that case, commit to first doing whatever you need to do to set it up (e.g., setting a reminder), then to biting the bullet when the time comes and actually getting it done. It may help if you remind yourself that people with interesting lives sometimes need to do the boring stuff too. By "interesting lives," I mean being able to pursue what is meaningful to them, not the kind of interesting that comes from panicked realizations and frantic scrambling. That's also pretty exciting, but in a more stressful way.

Don't Suffer More Than You Have To

Suffering comes not only from being in situations that we don't like, but also from what we tell ourselves about it. I'm not one of those annoying influencers who says that all you have to do is decide to be happy. That's a good idea taken too far, but there is some truth to it. Once you've done what you can to change your situation (like applying the strategies in the rest of the book), then what's left is acceptance. This doesn't mean that you're 100% happy about what's happening, but rather that you aren't going to burn a bunch of extra mental energy (and make the task worse) by complaining about how boring it is. Fully accepting that the task will be boring means not trying to fight it or let yourself complain about how boring it is. Probably no one would debate you on the boringness, so all that complaining and anger suggest you're subconsciously hanging on to the hope that being indignant will somehow change it. It won't.

By focusing on what you're unhappy about, you just feel more unhappy. This includes griping about what is unfair, unnecessary, redundant, poorly designed, annoying, and/or just plain dumb about what you need to do. The slippery

> This task may be mandatory, but suffering isn't.

slope is that the more right you are, the easier it is to feel justified in your complaints—and then trapped in your unhappiness. Remind yourself that part of the cost of a good life is sometimes doing things you hate, because it benefits your life in other ways.

Whistling while you work may be too big a stretch, but you can try to shift your focus. Maybe there's an aspect that is somewhat less annoying. Maybe focus on the next progress marker, whether by time (e.g., fifteen minutes done, forty-five to go!) or by accomplishment (e.g., halfway done!). Bring enough energy to keep pushing forward at a good pace rather than trudging through it—that only drags out your misery. Add other fun things, like music, podcasts, videos, call a friend, a new location, some sort of variation, or whatever will distract you enough while still allowing you to make progress.

Finally, make a point of reminding yourself of how good it will feel to know you did it. Look beyond the suffering of the present moment and put yourself into what it will feel like when you're done. Give yourself some credit for doing a pretty good job. Remind yourself that you can hold your head high without worry of being called out for not getting this done, and that you can confidently answer if anyone asks you about it. There's a freedom that comes from that.

Put It to Work

- What boring tasks are you avoiding? What price are you paying for that, both tangible and intangible? Does anyone else know what you're not getting to? Do they have any feelings about that?

- Write out how your life would be better when these dreaded tasks are done or at least done enough. How can you remind yourself of these rewards, as vividly as possible, when you don't want to do something?

- Identify how you can set yourself up to get to those dreaded tasks by making it easier to do the work or reducing the barriers to starting. How can you remind yourself of the benefits so that you keep setting yourself up for success?

- ## What, When, Where, and Why?

What strategies are you going to apply from this chapter? How will this be different from what you're already doing? Or perhaps have done before?

When and where? The more specific you can be, the better. Then actively look for these moments. Or set an alarm or other reminder to pull your attention to it. How can you set things up beforehand to make this easier to stick with?

Why? What problem will this solve or improve? What are all the direct and indirect benefits of this change? How is your life better for it? This is your motivation for when you don't feel like it.

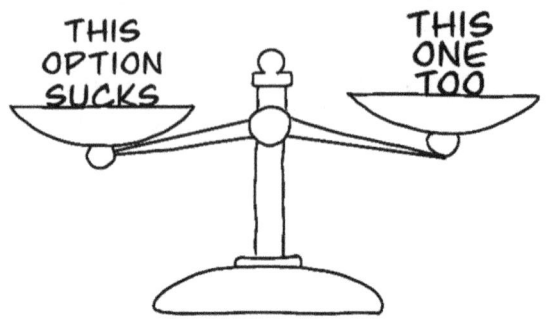

EENY MEANEY MINEY MOE?

25. Ambivalence: Pick a Side

WE CAN ALL HAVE MIXED feelings about a task that we want or need to do. Part of us wants to do it (or at least is willing), and another part of us would rather do something else. Most of the time, it isn't that close a call, so we decide to do the task or let it go. Fine. Life moves on, no looking back.

Sometimes, though, we get stuck, caught between doing and not doing. We feel ambivalent—part of us feels like we should do it, but another, equal, part really doesn't want to. These are the tasks that loiter on our to do list and make us curse a little every time we see them there. There's a certain kind of suffering that comes from these torn-in-two situations. It's different from what we feel about tasks that we might be procrastinating on but know we will eventually get to. We're ambivalent, and ambivalence involves more angsting when we really can't decide which way to go.

Being perfectionistic leaves you vulnerable to feeling stuck in ambivalence. If you set high standards, it can feel hard to hit the mark, so you hesitate to start but still feel the pressure to do the task. The pressure builds and builds, but you're still stuck in neutral. Really stressful.

Maybe You Only Feel Like You Should Do It

When I've had clients wrestle with ambivalence about a task, there's usually a part of them that feels like they should do the task, either because someone else told them to or because they're assuming that someone else really wants them to. It feels like an externally imposed obligation. Sometimes, just to make it worse, there's also a feeling that they should *want* to do the task even though they definitely don't.

We all have times when we act out of obligation but have accepted that we just need to do it. The task is boring or frustrating, but whatever. We don't feel torn about it though, so we find a way to slog through or at least do enough of it to be able to call it quits. When we are stuck in ambivalence, we haven't come to that acceptance. Or alternatively, we haven't accepted the cost of telling that other person no. So, we sweat in the middle, squeezed between the expectation and not wanting to meet it.

> Saying no is always an option if you're willing to pay the price.

If you have struggled to get things done, you may feel like you can't say no, that you owe it to the person to agree to this task even though you really don't want to or can't do it. Or you may worry about the social consequences if you say no because it will be yet another time when you disappoint them. This leaves you feeling trapped between guilt and your true desires, between being good to the other person and being good to yourself.

Can You Tip It One Way or the Other?

If you're feeling haunted by an unfinished task, step back and take a look at the two sides. Why should you do it? Why not? Make a really good case both ways. Maybe even write out your reasons on each side. While you're at it, write down any assumptions you might be making that affect how you feel about it, one way or the other. For example, you may be making assumptions about how good the end result needs to be or how awful the task will be to complete. In this case, it could be helpful to get more information about the task or desired outcome. As in, can you get some guidance that will make it easier to do? Or maybe find out how big a deal it would be to not complete it?

Ambivalence is all about that feeling of 50/50, that you can't decide either way. Maybe you can tip it one way or the other so it's easier to decide. You might try to make the task more of a winner. This might involve looking for ways to make the task less awful. For example, would a smaller production suffice? Or lower quality? Can you get someone to help you or maybe use a different process to pretty much get the job done—such as buying cupcakes for the bake sale instead of making them yourself? The less the job sucks, the less willpower it takes to get over that hump.

You can also make it a winner by pumping up the positives that come from completing it. What would it get you? Maybe you need to find out what you stand to gain from it. For example, how much could you potentially save by researching new car insurance? Above a certain point, it will be worth the hassle, so what's the potential upside?

You could also try to break the tie by deciding that the task is actually a loser that isn't worth the effort. This might involve accepting the consequences that will (or may) come from cutting that task loose. If there's a financial cost, you may decide that the money isn't worth the headache. Or maybe cutting the task loose involves disappointing someone who might try to pressure you to change your mind. That's not fun, but it may still be better than suffering through that dreaded task. It should also be noted that preemptively telling someone that you won't be doing something, hopefully with plenty of lead time, is a very different situation from dropping the ball by forgetting a commitment or by just not finishing it on time. The former involves making an active decision for yourself. The latter is letting your ADHD decide. The more you decide for yourself and are good about letting people know before the last minute, the easier it is to be assertive when it really matters.

Accept Still Being Torn

Sometimes people get stuck in ambivalence because they don't like either option and are hoping there is another way to resolve this that they will feel good about. Perfectionistic folks will hope for one clear winner so they don't need to worry about not choosing the other one (which is obviously terrible).

You may be able to tip that 50/50 into 60/40, but it's unlikely to ever get to 90/10 where you can go forth with a clean conscience. Probably you will be stuck with something closer to 51/49—enough to declare a winner but definitely not enough to feel good about it. Some decisions don't feel good, but that doesn't mean that they're the wrong ones. They're just the least bad—which is as good as it gets sometimes. Perhaps you've reached the point where it's unlikely there will be new information that would change your mind. Or maybe the deadline is upon you and it's go time. You may need to hold your nose while you choose, but just pull the trigger and move on. Then don't look back.

> Some decisions just feel bad, even when they're the right one.

Just Not Important Enough

You may have a collection of tasks that keep hanging in there between dumping and doing. You never actually get to them, but you feel like you can't just cut them loose. Every time you get close to doing them, some other, more important task takes your time. This is called *pseudo-procrastination*. It's easy to assume the problem is that you're not productive enough or that you're procrastinating on those tasks, but the real problem may be that these tasks are OK ideas but not actually good enough to make the cut. The solution is either to decide that they need a promotion or to just accept that you're never going to get to them. Either way, clear the decks so they don't clutter up your to do list.

Put It to Work

- Identify a few tasks that you're ambivalently stuck on. What are the two sides that you feel torn between? Would it help to write them all out? Which side has at least a slightly stronger case? Do you just need to pick one and move on?

- How can you make one of these ambivalent tasks easier or less awful so you can pick a side and move on? What standards can you lower or corners can you cut? What's good enough?

- Identify a task that you feel obligated to complete but just can't get going on. How can you explain to the other person that you are not going to do it? What response are you worried about and how could you handle that?

- ## What, When, Where, and Why?

What strategies are you going to apply from this chapter? How will this be different from what you're already doing? Or perhaps have done before?

When and where? The more specific you can be, the better. Then actively look for these moments. Or set an alarm or other reminder to pull your attention to it. How can you set things up beforehand to make this easier to stick with?

Why? What problem will this solve or improve? What are all the direct and indirect benefits of this change? How is your life better for it? This is your motivation for when you don't feel like it.

BEST
ORGANIZED
SOCK
DRAWER

26. No, That's Fake Productivity

B EING BUSY IS NOT THE same thing as being productive. Sure, it can look like it, but the real question is whether what you're doing is actually worth doing—versus just kind of worth doing. Sort of. At least eventually... OK, fine, I just couldn't make myself sort through all those health insurance claims.

Life is full of difficult, challenging, boring, and/or frustrating tasks that really are important. Fortunately and unfortunately, life is also full of tasks that may not be as important but are definitely less awful, so it's tempting to do these B-list activities as a way to avoid doing the tasks that require cognitive or emotional heavy lifting. See, I'm getting stuff done here! This feels much better than doing something that's indefensibly unproductive, like slack-jawed scrolling. The kind-of-beneficial activity gives us some cover, whether from our own guilty conscience or others' judgey opinions. In these moments, we're not aspiring to greatness, but we're also not totally wasting time—we walk the unobjectionable middle.

> Real productivity means finding a way to do the hardest jobs. Eventually.

Russell Ramsay, PhD has coined the term *procrastivity* for this procrastination via productivity. This is when we work on marginally productive tasks as a justification for procrastinating on more cognitively or emotionally demanding tasks. We all have times when we just can't muster the motivation or mental energy for the task that's hanging most heavily over our heads. Doing something easier could actually be the best we can get in that moment. Where procrastivity comes in is when it might be possible to bite the bullet but instead we let ourselves off the hook. It's more about avoidance of the harder in favor of the easier.

Life brings plenty of random excuses we can dive into, but we all probably have favorite procrastivity tasks that we use most. This could be something like checking email or other messaging, scanning the news, putting a few things away, etc. That feels good because we're staying on top of things. We're being responsive! We're doing our share! It may also be easier to click through messages than it is to do "real" work. At home, it could be things such as loading the dishwasher rather than staring into the fridge and figuring out how to cobble together a dinner that won't elicit a mutiny.

Be on the lookout for the times when you're sliding into procrastivity, when you're going towards the softball rather than what you really need to take a swing at. Here are some questions to ask yourself to figure out if you're taking the easy route:

- *Is this really what I should be doing now?* Could I make a good case for doing the easier task—a case that would convince someone else?

- *Am I doing this, or not doing something else?* The heart of procrastivity is that we're avoiding a harder task. We use the easier but still kind of productive task as a way to feel better about our choice.

- *Am I going towards something or away from something?* If you didn't have that harder task hanging over your head, would you still be doing that easier task, or is it only appealing by comparison?

As I've said before, you don't need to be a relentless productivity robot. It's fine to cruise in the right lane sometimes. The problem with procrastivity, when overdone, is that we then regret the consequences of that unfinished task. There may be time to do it later, but sometimes there isn't, at least not without some undesirable price.

To avoid these frustrating later moments, you need to accept and tolerate the discomfort of the harder task. In other words, you need to acknowledge that it won't be fun—it might even totally suck—but it will be worth it. You could easily find something more enjoyable to do instead, but you won't. Pump up your motivation by really reminding yourself of the benefits of biting the bullet now. How does it make your life better? How will you feel when you're finished and know you have done a good job? How does that feel compared to knowing you wiggled out again?

If you can't get yourself to commit to the whole job, can you at least talk yourself into starting? Just five minutes. Just see how it goes. At least gather up what you need for this task or figure out what you need to do next. Any little bit of progress can build momentum.

If you put up a good fight even though you couldn't get those wheels turning, it will be easier to walk away with your head held high. Work on that easier task instead and give yourself partial credit. Tomorrow is a new day.

Over-Thinking and Under-Doing

We should also take a minute to point out another form of fake productivity. Sometimes thinking about a task feels like we're doing something about it, especially if we're really burning mental energy on it. Maybe. Sometimes—if we're considering new information or perspectives and our thinking is going somewhere. This is that back-of-the-mind problem-solving that can come up with some great new ideas. But just ruminating on something isn't that. Going round and round in the same circles with the same information doesn't really move our understanding forward. This is especially true if it's mostly worrying or angsting, which bring suffering but not much to show for it.

However, because we're actively engaged with the problem, it can feel like we're doing *something* about it. This can even take on the role of a pressure release valve that drains off the motivation to act because we feel like we're working on it. This same thing can happen when we talk to others about the problem. And keep talking about it. This thinking and talking can take the place of real action towards a goal. And, of course, because no real progress has been made, this keeps the problem alive and gives us something to keep worrying about.

If you find yourself on this torturous merry-go-round, then take a few deep breaths and ask yourself what you can do that will actually move you forward on this goal. Maybe you need some new information. Maybe you just need to go with what you have, try some things, see what happens, and make adjustments. Maybe you need to spend less time thinking about this and actively slide your thoughts over to something better.

> Unfortunately, thinking about an anniversary gift doesn't necessarily round up to having one.

You probably need to accept that you won't enjoy the process, that it will be uncomfortable, but remind yourself that that's OK. You can handle uncomfortable. If you really feel stuck on it, go back and read *24. Just Bite the Bullet on Things You Hate.* If it feels like a relief to read another chapter rather than work on that dreaded project, then remind yourself that you will eventually need to apply what you learned there.

Put It to Work

- Identify your favorite procrastivity tasks and when you're most likely to use them. What makes them easier to do? What makes them feel kind of productive? How beneficial are they, really?

- Identify the tasks that you're most tempted to avoid with procrastivity tasks. What makes them so uncomfortable? How do you convince yourself that it's OK to delay getting to them? How much better would you feel if you were to just get them done?

- Notice those times that you're tempted to slide off onto a procrastivity task. How can you make the procrastivity tasks harder to jump into? What can you tell yourself to resist them? How can you make the avoided task easier to start?

- ## What, When, Where, and Why?

What strategies are you going to apply from this chapter? How will this be different from what you're already doing? Or perhaps have done before?

When and where? The more specific you can be, the better. Then actively look for these moments. Or set an alarm or other reminder to pull your attention to it. How can you set things up beforehand to make this easier to stick with?

Why? What problem will this solve or improve? What are all the direct and indirect benefits of this change? How is your life better for it? This is your motivation for when you don't feel like it.

THE CONVINCE-O-MATIC 2000

27. The Love and Hate of Deadlines

LIKE NIGHT FOLLOWS DAY, life brings deadlines. Time marches relentlessly forward whether we're paying attention or not. If noticing time isn't your superpower, then deadlines will probably stress you out a lot more, at least when they suddenly appear in your awareness (holy crap!). Folks with ADHD tend to be much more driven by close deadlines because far off deadlines really don't do much for them. It's much harder to internally generate the motivation beforehand—as in, "I don't *have to* work on this yet, but it would be good to chip away at it." This is why people with ADHD tend to procrastinate until the pressure of a more immediate deadline kicks them into action. I talk about why this is in *2. ADHD Makes It Harder to See Time* and *3. ADHD Makes It Harder to Feel the Future*.

If you struggle to get stuff done before the deadline is almost upon you, it leaves you vulnerable to the unexpected, especially if you also tend to underestimate how long things take. Or if you tend to be overly optimistic about how it will all come together. Even if you're totally cool with riding the rush of the last millisecond, you may find that some people in your life get really angsty that you haven't yet sprung into action. I have a saying that ADHD can cause anxiety, but it's not always in the person with ADHD. While we could take the position that it isn't your job to manage other people's anxiety, it is your job to not provoke behavior from others that you don't want, such as nagging, lecturing, and general freaking out.

This is especially important if you tend to have a bit of an oppositional streak. (No judgment, I get it.) While it is definitely true that there are controlling micromanagers out there, it is also true that being kind of cavalier about others' deadlines tends to invite more managing. You may even find that you get into a mental tug of war with your own deadlines. And also that a tug of war is way more exciting than doing the task but is just another form of procrastination.

> **Persistence gets you somewhere. Stubbornness keeps you stuck.**

If you feel yourself digging in, take a moment to remind yourself that no one can make you do anything since they can't move your body. They may threaten or bribe, but you're still the one who decides whether to do it. If you do it, it's because you decided that you prefer the benefits of doing the task over the cost of not—that's agency and self-determination. You're in charge.

We might wish we had some different options, but we choose among the options that are available. For example, we're not required to pay our bills on time or even at all, but if we're late then we accept the extra fees, and if we try to skip out entirely then we accept that it may end in court. We make the choices that we do because we assume that it will work out better for us. Complaining about a deadline or a task that we don't want to do may make us feel better in the moment but doesn't change our options. If you really don't want to do something, then either accept the cost or have a direct conversation with whoever is imposing the deadline and try to convince them to let you off the hook.

Honor the (Real) Deadline

Soft deadlines are demotivating—especially with ADHD. Vague, open deadlines are basically a get out of jail free card. In my many conversations about productivity, I've noticed that sometimes people preemptively let themselves off the hook by intentionally leaving a deadline soft. This is different from deciding to put a deadline on hold for now, until you get to a point where you can decide what to do about it. Instead, what I'm talking about here is knowing in the back of our head that we're not really committed to this task, but we don't want to come out and admit it. So, we let it sit in limbo with a soft deadline. I've seen this with tasks that someone feels like they should want to do but just don't, but they don't yet want to cut it loose. I've also seen this with bedtimes where they know they should set an earlier time, but they enjoy their nights so they purposely leave it unspecified (with predictable results that night and the next morning).

If you're serious about getting something done, then it needs a real deadline. As in, a specific time that has some possibility of happening. This also requires investing the cognitive effort to determine what the real deadline should be—and whether it's even possible given everything else (which, annoyingly, requires knowing everything else you need to do). In other words, it can be a lot of work to not only hit the deadline, but even to decide what it should be.

All of this still applies if it's someone else's deadline for you. If they leave it vague, you're probably much less likely to hit the mark, if there even is one. Or perhaps they're clear on the deadline, but for some reason you're not. You may feel embarrassed to ask, assuming they told you but you forgot—you know, given that this has happened once or twice. While they may be a little annoyed that you forgot, they will almost certainly be more annoyed if you miss the deadline, so asking is almost always better than guessing. And, by the way, your little secret of not knowing the deadline will be revealed anyway when you look surprised when

> It's best to show people that you care, but if you can't show them, then tell them.

they ask if you're done. If you don't believe the deadline they gave you or if you're not sure you can do it on their proposed timeline, then talk about it directly right when they give it to you. Or as soon as you realize there will be a problem. You may worry about being held to that new time, but it will look much better than them assuming you missed the

original deadline because you just didn't care enough.

Plan to Procrastinate

You may find it helpful sometimes to go with your ADHD tide rather than fight it. You can do this by planning to procrastinate. That is, by blocking out time in your schedule right before the deadline to work on the task. This way you don't forget about it or double-book yourself or mistakenly believe that you have extra time there. If you later have a schedule conflict, you can move this block of work time around, but at least that amount of time is claimed.

Planning to procrastinate works best when you can roughly predict how long the task will take so you don't find yourself short. It also works best when you're pretty confident that other random emergencies won't blow up—and you're willing to take that chance. If these criteria are true, then you can use that deadline pressure to its best effect.

Feel the Deadline Earlier

Big jobs with far off deadlines are really hard to motivate for beforehand and really hard to complete at the last minute, even though you want to think that you can—college freshmen often learn this the hard way. I'm definitely not going to say that it will be easy to make yourself work ahead on projects that you know aren't due right now. Other than asking people to lie to you about the real deadline, it will take some intentional effort to set yourself up for success, and then even more intentional effort to make yourself do it when the time comes.

Start by creating some interim deadlines for parts of the project. Yeah, I know you've known this since middle school, but this is still the first step. Here's the harder next part—actually schedule times to work on those interim deadlines. As in, pull out your schedule and sprinkle in blocks of time to hammer away at them. The hardest part is yet to come, which is doing the actual work in those scheduled moments. But if you have it scheduled, then at least there's a better chance that something might happen. Let's all be honest—it's still far from a guarantee, but it's better than the zero percent chance if you don't plan the time.

So, how do you convert this idealistic thought into real action? There are a lot of strategies that you can use, some of which I cover in *20. And Probably a To Do List, Too*. For example, plan these times earlier in the day so they don't get pushed out as new things pop up. You can also use some external accountability by telling someone that you're going to work on it at that time. For bonus points (and if it won't make things weird), you could even ask them to ask you if you did it. Preferably, this is someone who can tell when you're lying. You can also set up regular check-ins with colleagues, your boss, romantic partner, or friend, depending on what kind of a project it is. This tends to work better if they have some skin in the game on you completing the project on time (as long they're not super neurotic about it because then they're just going to annoy you). There are even websites that set up accountability pairings with strangers where you tell each other what you will work on and then check in at the end. Even this little extra nudge can make a difference.

It's also helpful to just generally manage your distractions and temptations before and during the time that you're supposed to be working ahead so that your attention doesn't grab onto something more fun. Also try to get enough sleep, work out, and eat well so you're bringing your A game. Probably flossing also fits in here somewhere. In other words, do all the stuff in the rest of this book. No wonder productivity is so hard...

Put It to Work

- How do deadlines bring out your oppositional behavior? What does that feeling remind you of? What price do you pay for digging your feet in on a deadline that you don't feel like working on?

- Notice how soft deadlines lead to lots of creep. What is the final price paid? How can you remind yourself of this earlier in the process? Invest the energy to figure out a real deadline.

- Pick a long-term project and break it into interim deadlines. How can you set yourself up to do the work along the way rather than all at the end? How can you feel the future benefits of working on this now to motivate yourself into action? How can you push more tempting distractions further away?

- ## What, When, Where, and Why?

What strategies are you going to apply from this chapter? How will this be different from what you're already doing? Or perhaps have done before?

When and where? The more specific you can be, the better. Then actively look for these moments. Or set an alarm or other reminder to pull your attention to it. How can you set things up beforehand to make this easier to stick with?

Why? What problem will this solve or improve? What are all the direct and indirect benefits of this change? How is your life better for it? This is your motivation for when you don't feel like it.

28. How Perfect Does That Need to Be?

A H, THE SWEET TEMPTATION OF perfection, of creating something that is beyond reproach and guaranteed to earn praise.

Sounds good, right?

It is, except that (1) nothing is ever actually that good, and (2) it probably isn't worth all the extra effort. For most things in life, good enough is good enough. Perfectionism is a way of managing anxiety related to uncertainty, self-doubt, or insecurity. Like many less-than-optimal coping mechanisms, it carries a high cost and doesn't actually work as well as promised. Treatment involves examining some of the beliefs behind those expensively high standards and building emotional muscle to tolerate uncertainty and others' judgment (real or imagined).

> Perfection is much nicer in theory than reality. And rarely achievable.

If undiagnosed ADHD gave you way too many experiences of being criticized for falling short, you may be extra sensitive to others' opinions. Obviously. As my friend Kristen Carder shares, "As someone with ADHD, it actually feels *unsafe* to be imperfect, even if it's with stuff that doesn't logically matter in the long run. So, there's a lot of emotion to wade through here." It can feel really important to protect yourself from not only the tangible consequences of missing the mark (like failing a test), but also from others' judgment, which might actually feel worse. It would then feel reasonable to overdo things just to make sure that what you produce is good enough. There's too high a cost for disappointing people, so perfectionism offers the promise of safety even if it's expensive in time and physical and mental energy.

All of this extra work is part of the cost of undiagnosed ADHD. Unfortunately, it also hides (sort of) the symptoms of ADHD, which can delay getting diagnosed—at least with ADHD. Getting diagnosed with anxiety and depression is pretty easy. By looking at your level of performance, at least what it looks like from the outside, a clinician might conclude that you don't have ADHD if they don't consider what it takes for you to (mostly) get everything done. This is especially likely if you're a woman who looks as if you have it all together (if they only knew...).

The positive ending to this painful story is that addressing your ADHD should make it easier to hit the mark with less effort. It will also make your performance more predictable and consistent so there's less worry about whether everything will come together this time or that you already forgot something that you're going to get ripped for tomorrow. Of course, knowing that your performance has improved is the (easier) cognitive part. There's also the emotional part—you need to believe that you're doing a better job, to really feel this improvement, to let go of perfectionism's protective benefits. This means feeling the discomfort of doing something good enough and then moving on. It also means accepting that sometimes someone will still be disappointed with you and that you'll need to be able to tolerate that discomfort without jumping back to the old habit of perfectionism.

You may find it helpful to talk to others who have had similar experiences of working extra hard to hide their ADHD—and preferably have come through to a more balanced perspective. This might be someone who is already in your life or someone you meet in an ADHD support setting, whether in person or online. Don't underestimate the power of connecting with others. You may find it reassuring to hear how things are working out for them. If you still find it too difficult to get that perfectionism monkey off your back, a therapist can help you tolerate those uncomfortable feelings and feel more confident in yourself.

Pseudo-Perfectionism

ADHD can also lead to, if not true perfectionism, then at least overdoing a task. As in, making it much bigger or better than it really needs to be. This can happen in a few ways. Getting hyperfocused on a task is a really good way to overshoot the mark if you lose track of time and spend too long on it or lose track of the purpose of the task in the first place. For example, spending an extra hour prettying up the spreadsheet that really just needed correct numbers. I have also seen clients who somewhat intentionally overdo the task as a way to crank up some motivation for it—a standard spreadsheet is really boring, but check out these animated graphs! And how 'bout that formatting!

Overdoing a task can also be a form of procrastivity, of working on something that's kind of productive as a way to avoid working on something that's more important but harder. (See *26. No, That's Fake Productivity* for more on this.) The extra time spent on a project delays biting the bullet on what else you should be working on.

Overdoing a task can also be an attempt to compensate for prior sins—for example, if you didn't do a great job on your last report or it was late, so you want to make this next one even better. On the one hand, it's smart to be aware of your reputation and to keep a fair balance in your relationships. Sometimes you do need to go that extra mile. On the other hand, do you actually? As in, did the other person tell you to make this next one even better? Or are you just feeling guilty and self-imposing this higher standard? Also, will overdoing this one burn up time that thereby takes away from other, worthier tasks?

Eyes on the Prize

It's important to feel like we do a good job on things, to feel competent and effective. We're told we should try hard and bring our best to everything we do. And yet, we only have so much energy in a day. We need to figure out how to dole it out among all the demands placed upon us—and also among the things that we just want to do. Ultimately, energy and time are zero-sum, so be sure that you have enough for what really matters to you.

If you're prone to perfectionism-lite or overdoing things, try to get some perspective on what you're doing and why. Where does this task fit relative to other demands? And where will the time to crank up the quality on this task come from, since every minute on this is a minute not available for anything else? To figure this out takes cognitive effort—and knowing what else is waiting for you. It's easier to just put our head down and run with whatever is right in front of us, but that may not be the best use of our time. Feels good in the moment, but doesn't feel great later.

If you feel like someone else is setting a high bar for you, then take a moment to get clear on what the other person wants and why. Does it need to be that good or would something quicker do the trick? You may be hesitant to ask because it may look like you're weaseling out of the work, but instead frame it as wanting to give them something that works while also making good use of your time—which is a good sales pitch if you have other things they want you to work on. Depending on the power dynamics, you may have some negotiating leverage to offer something that works better for you, but you may not feel like you're allowed to assert yourself if you feel like you let people down too often.

If you too often feel like you owe someone something extra or maybe aren't sure how to navigate others' expectations, I have good news: I have an entire section on that: *VII. The Social Side of Productivity*. You owe it to yourself to read it.

Everything Needs to Be Just Right

Most of the time when we talk about perfectionism, it's about the end result. However, there is also a kind of perfectionism that some folks with ADHD fall into which is the belief that the circumstances need to be just right for them to get anything done. If anything is less than ideal, then it can feel like a roadblock to making any progress. Granted, folks with ADHD may be more sensitive to the situation they're working in as well as their own internal state and therefore more vulnerable to getting knocked off track when something is off. This is true, but not 100% true in a black and white way. The more nuanced statement is that you may need to use more willpower to get going and stay on track when things aren't just right, but you can still make some progress.

This is important because perfect circumstances are pretty hard to come by, which makes for a lot of lost time if you feel like you need to wait until all the stars align. Maybe it isn't your best work, but maybe it's as good as it needs to be. Or it gives you something to polish up later, which is less work than starting from scratch.

If you find yourself leaning into this idea that the circumstances aren't right enough and that therefore you can't get anything done, then push yourself to run a little experiment. Is there something you can start working on that will in some way move this project along? Can you go back and edit or review what you've already done? Can you jump back in where you left off, even if progress is slower and you're not electrified with inspiration? Can you jot down some notes for yourself for what needs to be done later? If you're able to make some meaningful contribution, then it proves that you don't need everything to be perfect. And if, this time, you just can't get it going, then you can go screw around knowing that at least you tried.

> Some progress, any progress, is better than no progress. Sometimes going for the gold just means showing up.

Put It to Work

- Identify the types of tasks or situations where you might overdo it. What are the thoughts and feelings that drive that? How well does perfectionism reduce that discomfort? And what does it take to create perfection? Is it worth it?

- When thinking about how good something needs to be, do you worry about what others might think about your performance—or you? How much effort does it take to minimize that anxiety? What can you tell yourself to better tolerate the discomfort that comes from risking others' judgment?

- Where do you shoot yourself in the foot in the worst ways? How can you stay more on top of demands so you don't feel like you owe too much? What conversations do you need to have to change people's expectations?

- ## What, When, Where, and Why?

What strategies are you going to apply from this chapter? How will this be different from what you're already doing? Or perhaps have done before?

When and where? The more specific you can be, the better. Then actively look for these moments. Or set an alarm or other reminder to pull your attention to it. How can you set things up beforehand to make this easier to stick with?

Why? What problem will this solve or improve? What are all the direct and indirect benefits of this change? How is your life better for it? This is your motivation for when you don't feel like it.

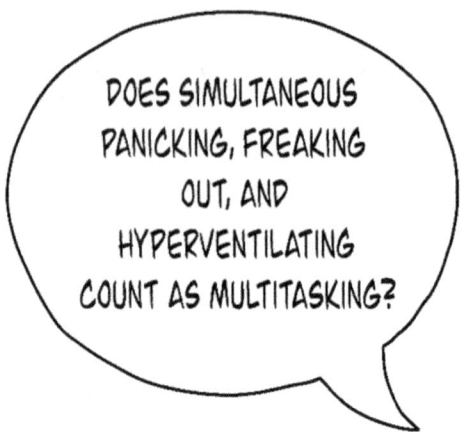

29. Overwhelm: Break Down Big Tasks

SOME TASKS FEEL TOO BIG to fit into your brain. Or it makes your brain hurt trying to cram it all in at the same time. Or maybe the task is too vague, confusing, complicated, frustrating... It just makes you want to run away and change your name. Cognitive overload leads to emotional overwhelm, so let's wind that back by starting with a few deep breaths to calm that fight or flight response before you try to wrap your brain around it all.

Once your heartrate dips back into the double digits, turn your attention back to figuring out what you need to do here. Invest the cognitive effort to start breaking it down. Highlight key points. Scribble in the margins. Stand up and walk around while talking aloud to yourself. Get out the necessary items and start moving them around. Call a friend for some advice. In general, it's probably helpful to download as much information out of your head as you can. Get it down onto paper or a screen. Separate out the different parts into piles. Color code stuff. Mark it up. Cross out what isn't important. The less you need to hold in your working memory, the more processing power you have left for actually thinking about the task. As my friend Nachi (Mike) Felt, PhD says, "it's all about creating clarity."

Oh right, this is going to be hard and you're going to hate it. But probably mostly in the beginning, until you begin to figure it out. We tend to assume that the strong feelings of the moment will last a lot longer than they usually do, so if you can stick in there, it will probably get better, especially if you feel like you're making some progress, instead of feeling so hopeless or overwhelmed. Therefore, commit to give it five minutes. Five measly minutes. Three hundred tiny little seconds. Hell, you can do anything for five minutes, right? Except hold your breath.

> Many overwhelming projects aren't necessarily harder; they just have more moving parts.

Start By Starting

Sometimes the best way to start something is to just start it. (Definitely highlight that last sentence.) The starting doesn't get any easier by waiting, so just start it now. Your future self, who is working on the cushy middle, will thank you for your sacrifice. So, where to begin?

If this task is coming from someone else, do you need to clarify their expectations or requirements? And maybe talk them down a little if it feels like too much? Even if the task is yours, can you reach out to someone else to get some advice, clarity, or direction? I'm a big fan of not re-inventing the wheel (a.k.a., I hate wasting my time) and am very happy to ask someone who knows better. Being willing to ask for help and knowing the right person to ask are important productivity skills.

Sometimes not knowing where to begin can cause someone to feel stuck. I have two recommendations. First, does it matter where you start? Sometimes it does, so figuring that out becomes your first job. But also, often it may not matter and the reason why you can't figure out where to start is that there really isn't a clear answer—there are a bunch of places that are all pretty good. In this case, just pick something and go. If it turns out not to be the best first step, then you'll figure

213

that out and can re-adjust. It may be that you couldn't know this until you've jumped in. This isn't impulsivity, it's experimenting.

This brings me to my second recommendation: have faith in the process. In other words, have faith that you'll figure it out, that experience is the best teacher, and that that feedback will help you understand better what to do next. Sitting and staring at it will only take you so far—but will burn up a ton of time if you let it. Unless it's something you can't undo (e.g., nuclear bombs, face tattoos), give yourself some permission to experiment. This isn't making mistakes, it's learning. It's creating wisdom.

> Pools don't get any warmer by walking around them.

You may also find that breaking a big job down into steps/phases is the first step. Or determining your contingencies—what do you need to know in order to make the next decision? What needs to happen before what else? This is kind of like creating an outline with your main checkpoints in order and then filling in the smaller steps under each of those.

Start at the End

Sometimes starting at the end is the better way to go—and not just because you're being oppositional. It may be that there is a specific end point that you're trying to get to, and you need to work backwards from that. Do you know where to end up? To fine-tune that answer, you may want to consider these questions:

- Why am I doing this?

- What problem does this solve or purpose does it serve? Why does this matter?

- What does success look like?

- What's the problem if I don't do it?

Before leaping into action, invest the time to get a clear direction—including on what you don't actually need to do. As good as it feels to get things done, it isn't actually progress if it isn't what you need to do (i.e., turns out that reading the directions is sometimes useful).

Make the Job Easier

Sometimes a job feels overwhelming because there are way too many options or things to think about and you can't consider eight million things all at once. For example, when I needed to buy a new laptop, the websites became overwhelming almost immediately as I started looking at different specs, manufacturers, and product numbers. I'm not depending on my computer to safely get me to Mars, so I quickly cut the infinity of options down by making a few specific decisions—operating system, processing speed, RAM, price range, and only two manufacturers. I accepted that there might be slightly better options I would miss, but it wasn't worth all the extra time and angst to sort through. Again, my computer just needs to be good enough. Then, within that smaller range, I narrowed down further and finally just picked something. It may not have been the 100% best computer for the absolute best price, but I didn't care—moving on.

Making a few key decisions can helpfully constrain your options to a more manageable number. Are there a few criteria that matter the most? Start there. If not, you may need to just arbitrarily make some decisions. If nothing stands out as the most important, then it means that everything is equally important—and equally unimportant. If you really can't decide, then do eeny, meeny, miney, moe. If you hate what you wound up with, great! Now you know better what to pick instead.

Put It to Work

- Think of a project that started out overwhelming, but you figured it out. How did you do that? What lessons can you remind yourself of for future overwhelming projects?

- Identify how you could externalize information for upcoming large projects so trying to keep it all in your head is less confusing. Remind yourself how this reduces the number of dropped details.

- Identify a current large project that feels overwhelming. How can you break it into more manageable parts? What are some early decisions that would helpfully reduce your other options?

- ## What, When, Where, and Why?

What strategies are you going to apply from this chapter? How will this be different from what you're already doing? Or perhaps have done before?

When and where? The more specific you can be, the better. Then actively look for these moments. Or set an alarm or other reminder to pull your attention to it. How can you set things up beforehand to make this easier to stick with?

Why? What problem will this solve or improve? What are all the direct and indirect benefits of this change? How is your life better for it? This is your motivation for when you don't feel like it.

30. Ambiguity: What Am I Supposed to Do Here?

IN THE LAST CHAPTER, we discussed overwhelm, where you perhaps are trying to juggle too much information. In this chapter, we will discuss the perhaps opposite situation, where you don't have enough information to create a clear sense of what you're supposed to do. Alternatively, you might need to make sense of the information you do have so you can figure out what else you need. When it comes to quantities of information, Goldilocks had it right—not too much, not too little, but just right.

ADHD can drive procrastination in several ways, but it's universal that ambiguity also drives procrastination. For example, if you're not sure:

- What needs to be done
- How it needs to be done
- The purpose it serves
- The desired endpoint

- When it needs to be done or how long you should spend on it

If you don't know what target you're shooting at, it's hard to know what to do. And feeling squeezed by the pressure of expectation without sufficient information is really stressful, so it's tempting to avoid dealing with it, at least right now. And now. And also now...

This is especially true if you are worried that the lack of information is your fault, that somehow you missed something important or forgot it. You may feel self-conscious about asking, worried that you will out your distractibility or forgetfulness. In your defense, there might have been situations where it was on you for missing it, and also definitely there have been people who made you feel like crap about that. Obviously, you would prefer not to have that experience yet again, so it can feel better to try to just figure it out on your own. This might be the best way to go—except when it's not possible, which can leave you feeling trapped. Having all the extra time to do it yourself may feel only slightly better than the embarrassment of asking. All of this is a really disempowering place to be, so distracting yourself from it is even more tempting. Unfortunately, more time passing tends to increase the pressure. Of course, sometimes the missing information somehow is randomly revealed and you're saved. Phew! Those times when you got lucky can make it easier to justify waiting this time, even when the odds of a miracle are pretty low.

Clarify the Unclear

If you're not sure what you're supposed to do, then getting clear on that is actually the first thing to do. This means coming up with some answers to the questions in the bullet list above by investing the cognitive effort to go through what you do know and to make sense of it all, to begin putting some pieces together and make some decisions. This might involve diving into the deep end, flailing around in a bunch of stuff that doesn't make sense, and having faith that your brain will create some order from the chaos—because it naturally tends to. This is what happened when I needed to buy a laptop—all those confusing specs and features began to fall into place. Lots of things don't make sense until they do, either gradually or in a flash of realization. You just need to stick in long enough for the magic to happen.

In addition to the cognitive effort, you may also need to invest the emotional effort to tolerate the discomfort of feeling lost at sea. Like with so many other important moments in life, the challenge is to go towards that discomfort, not away. Whether physical or emotional, discomfort is often a helpful warning sign that alerts us to potential trouble, which is mostly helpful—except when it isn't. In this case, feeling confused and unsure is accurate and what you're supposed to feel when you don't understand something. None of this means there's a problem here or that you can't figure it out if you hang in there. Invoke your oppositional streak and frame it as a challenge. Or make it an interesting mystery to solve. Just be sure to remind yourself that it's supposed to be hard, that struggling isn't a problem, and that you just need to last slightly longer than the confusion does.

You may want to jump in with something of an intentional plan or methodical process if you have one, but even that may be a step ahead of where you are. Fine. Maybe you just need to dive in and see where it takes you, to see what emerges from the fog.

If the whole thing feels too vague, you may want to bite the bullet and make some decisions, such as what parts of it you will focus on, prioritize, or ignore. This chops it down to a more manageable pile of information.

If you're really not sure what to do or if it's taking too long to figure it all out, who can you ask? Does someone have a key piece of information that will make a big difference? Or maybe they just have the experience that will save you a lot of headache. If it's your boss or a customer, they may have some preferences that would be really good to know. Even if they told you before, they will probably see your asking as indicating your diligence rather than your forgetfulness. Even if asking does

> It's almost always better to ask than to guess.

reveal your forgetting, it's still way better to be seen as a diligent forgetter than an irresponsible one. If you're tempted to just take your chances, remind yourself that missing the mark kind of spills the beans, too.

Besides the obvious direct benefits of whatever you're trying to accomplish, it might be that the indirect benefits of feeling good about yourself for hanging in there are actually more important. This might be especially true if decades of struggling with undiagnosed ADHD have caused you to doubt not only your intelligence to figure it out, but also your perseverance to hang in there. Decades of trying only to fall short *again*, without a clear understanding as to why or what to do about it, makes it easy to be pessimistic that it will work out any differently this time.

This is what can be so transformational about an ADHD diagnosis—it enables you to apply your abilities more consistently, so you can have more faith that hanging in there will be worth the effort. It enables you to believe in yourself in a way that you never could before. Now you have a decent shot at figuring out this ambiguous, confusing, messy project. Now you have a reason to believe in not only your ability to figure it out, but also your ability to hang in there long enough to do so.

Put It to Work

- Identify what feelings or insecurities ambiguity brings up for you. How do you tend to respond? How would you prefer to respond instead?

- Create a list of things to tell yourself when you're tempted to avoid clarifying ambiguity or it feels like too much work. What would be most convincing?

- Identify one current task or project where ambiguity is holding you back. What next step can begin to create some clarity and get you moving?

- ## What, When, Where, and Why?

What strategies are you going to apply from this chapter? How will this be different from what you're already doing? Or perhaps have done before?

When and where? The more specific you can be, the better. Then actively look for these moments. Or set an alarm or other reminder to pull your attention to it. How can you set things up beforehand to make this easier to stick with?

Why? What problem will this solve or improve? What are all the direct and indirect benefits of this change? How is your life better for it? This is your motivation for when you don't feel like it.

SECTION VII. THE SOCIAL SIDE OF PRODUCTIVITY

OTHER PEOPLE WILL HAVE THOUGHTS and feelings not only about what you do, but also about how you do it. And also definitely when. Sometimes these people have a direct stake in what you're doing, like a spouse or coworker. But even if they don't, they may still have some strong opinions that carry social implications for you. Therefore, we can't really talk about productivity without also talking about how you navigate other people's expectations.

ADHD can make it harder to be the person that you want to be, to do what you hope to, and to show what you're capable of. Just as it can make you doubt yourself, it can really make others doubt you. As much as I might hope that you learn to be so productive that you never disappoint anyone again, that's not possible because some people have unrealistic expectations, regardless of what you do. More to the point, it may not be worth it to you to meet their expectations, even if you could. A history of negative experiences with dropping the ball may muddy these situations, making it harder to sort out what you want versus what others might want of you. You may also be unsure about whether it will make things better or worse to disclose your ADHD.

There's a lot in life that doesn't have definitive answers. How you should handle other people's expectations is definitely one of them. That said, there are some wise guiding principles that will help you balance your needs with others'.

31. Social Pressure, Faking It, and Falling Short

THOSE ADHD MOMENTS SURE CAN add up. Everyone has their moments, but if you aren't managing your ADHD well (say, for several decades before being diagnosed), then you will have more of those moments. Like, a lot more. Despite great intentions and vehement proclamations to yourself and others that this time will be different... unfortunately, not so different. Having ADHD means using up your free passes too quickly and then people start noticing. If you're lucky, they also notice that you seem to work really hard and that you feel worse when you drop the ball than they do. If you're unlucky, they make assumptions about why you didn't hit the mark, mostly that you should have tried harder.

Once you've had a couple million of these situations where you feel judged, you may start judging yourself and look to trying harder as your salvation. It seems logical, right? It should work, shouldn't it? The irony, of course, is that you're probably already working harder, it's just not translating into enough results, at least not at the right times. Even when you do do a good job, you may feel bad about how you got there (if they only knew…) or even assume that someone else probably would have done it better. Knocking down your successes like this gives you defeats when you could use some victories.

There's also always the potential for those ticking time bombs, the stuff that someone expects of you that totally fell off your radar—but definitely not off theirs. ADHD makes it easy to worry about what you don't know you don't know. Maybe you missed the email. Maybe you said you would do it but then totally forgot. Maybe something was mentioned in one of those meetings. This is a special kind of self-torture because these fears are impossible to disprove. Even if you slowly click through your entire inbox and all your texts, maybe you agreed in a conversation. Even if you rack your brain, maybe there's no trace at all—until suddenly someone's mad that you missed the deadline. Damnit! This ever-present worry puts you in a defensive position and unlevels the playing field.

A More Nuanced Discussion of Masking

Masking has become a popular term in the world of ADHD and even more so in the world of autism. It refers to the extra energy that some people have to expend to "look normal." As in, not neurodivergent. This could be things like setting a bunch of reminders to not forget, working really hard to not interrupt people, or needing to be hyper-organized because otherwise it all goes to hell. Other people who have other struggles will likely feel pressure to mask in different ways. It is often discussed as yet another cost of being different in a society that doesn't understand or accept that we don't all function the same. This disconnect between abilities and expectations can lead to fatigue, burnout, depression, and low self-esteem.

Like so much else that blows up on social media, there's something to this, but too often it is also over-simplified in a way that I don't think is helpful to the people who need it most. So, let's start with the big picture. We all engage in some degree of doing what we think is expected of us. We read the room and adapt our behavior. We do this all the time as we navigate social situations where each person has different preferences and agendas. I say this as a joke, but if I was 100% true to myself and said every single thing I thought, I would be divorced, and if I did every single thing I wanted to, I would be in jail. We all edit our behavior all the time.

We live in a society where people's actions affect others and everyone has expectations of how they think others should behave. It's messy and some people definitely get misinterpreted and screwed, in big and small ways. But this editing is what it takes for society to operate... to the extent that it does.

Hopefully you live and work with people who get you or are at least open enough to you being honest with them about what you need. Hopefully when you let down the mask, they are decent about what they see and willing to give you a little something—like politely holding up their hand when you interrupt, so they can keep talking. Everybody does their part and everybody benefits. They feel less resentful and you feel less guilty. This is much less work and probably leaves both people with more trust in the relationship.

Where masking becomes a problem is when someone feels like they can't be themselves because there is something wrong with who they are. Or when they feel like they need to work ten times as hard to "do the normal stuff everyone else just does" so no one finds out how screwed up they are. In this case, the problem is this belief that different = defective. (Tell yourself out loud that "different isn't defective." Say it again. Do you believe it?) It may also be a problem that that belief was so easy to come to because that person had been told so often by others that they are, in fact, defective. Obviously, this is not OK.

We all need to function in the world that we live in, complete with other people's sometimes unfair, misguided, ill-informed, or just plain mean-spirited ideas. People are allowed to have their opinions, but equally, you're allowed to not take them personally. You may choose to address it in an assertive but still respectful way—some people just need to be educated. Or at least are willing to kind of go along with what you're asking for. That's fine. Maybe it will sink in later. If someone seems less judgmental, you may choose to let the mask down a bit and ask for what would make for a better situation.

> The more secure you are in who you are, the less affected you will be by others' opinions.

Effective assertiveness is an important skill, but we can't fight every battle. We all (hopefully) want more acceptance for diversity of all kinds, but there will be some people or situations where it doesn't seem worth the fight. That's not a comment on you or how you deserve to be treated, but rather is an assessment of the likely outcome of addressing it. You may wisely choose that here, in this situation in your life, that you don't want to be the one who winds up getting treated worse for a worthy cause. It may be much wiser to let this moment of injustice or maybe just misunderstanding go by because it isn't worth it *to you*. No matter how right you are, confronting the situation may not leave you happy or better off. This doesn't mean that others' bad behavior is acceptable. Don't feel bad about yourself, and definitely don't let other people tell you who you are. Hold your head high and see yourself as a wise warrior who will come back tomorrow. Remind yourself that you have lots of friends out there who do appreciate and get you and who you can be yourself around.

Earn Back Some Social Capital

We earn good standing in our relationships through good deeds—what we do, but also how we do things and generally treat the other person. This is called *social capital*. If you feel like your ADHD sometimes affects your ability to meet others' expectations, then it costs you some of that social capital. It may also cost you actual capital, like if you tell your friend you will buy them a drink because you were late—you exchange money into the lost social capital. It also helps if the other person knows that your being late isn't for lack of trying and understands that this is part of the package deal of your friendship or work relationship, and that they appreciate the rest of what you bring.

Of course, rather than always making up for these losses or hoping that your charm will win the day, you can also protect your social capital by doing a better job of managing your ADHD and generally being more productive. While it may be a stretch to call this book *How to Win Friends and Influence People for ADHDers*, we could probably call it *How to Not Piss People Off*, but probably shouldn't. Not pissing people off is a pretty low bar, and it feels terrible when you're under that bar. The goal is to get your ADHD managed enough that it doesn't take too much away from everything that's awesome and worth appreciating about you.

We should also point out that there is an important second way to not disappoint people—being wise about what you take on in the first place will also reduce your

ADHD moments. Slowing down before agreeing to do something and really thinking about whether you can do it or even want to will spare you uncomfortable moments later. You may also want to hedge your bets and set the right expectations beforehand rather than explain your shortcoming later.

You may also find it helpful to disclose your ADHD if it's the right situation and the right person. Since this decision may be more nuanced than you might think, I have two whole chapters on this: *33. Should You Tell People You Have ADHD?* and *34. What About Disclosing at Work?*

We should also point out that sometimes the problem isn't your ADHD, but rather the other person's expectations, including for what treatment will change. If they secretly, or not so secretly, expect you to become just like them, it's not going to work out. The problem is the mismatch between what happens and what they're hoping for. While it may be beneficial in a number of ways for you to up your batting average, there will come a point where the

> Don't set me up for failure and you up for disappointment.

other person needs to decide whether they can flex their expectations to meet you halfway—or continue to be unhappy. There may also come a point where you decide that their disappointed expectations aren't your problem to fix.

A Strong Core

Poorly managed ADHD makes life too much about avoiding negatives, including socially. You should aspire for more. What are the positives that you want to pursue in your various relationships? How would things be better and what would be possible if you felt like an equal rather than like you always kind of owe people a little something? How would you show up differently? How would you feel about what happens then? For example, you may feel more confident about putting your ideas out in team meetings. Or you could join the group for lunch rather than holding back and (hopefully) working through.

The obvious part of earning this stronger social position is to use all the good strategies from this book and elsewhere. But the equally important other half is to make a point of noticing and giving yourself credit for all the good things that you do. If you ignore or dismiss that good effort, you'll keep yourself in the weaker social position. Even if that good effort wasn't enough to prevent an ADHD moment, still give yourself credit for what you did do so you're more motivated to do it again next time. Partial credit totally counts since maybe the outcome will go the other way next time.

This balanced perspective makes it possible to own your mistakes without falling apart. First own it, then fix it. What can you do at this point to address what didn't work out and the social fallout from it? Nothing earns back respect like looking mistakes dead in the eye.

> Define yourself not by what you struggle most with, but by your best.

Put It to Work

- Reflect on how the impact of ADHD on your productivity has influenced how you see yourself overall. What can you expect of yourself? What do you deserve? What can you ask of others?

- Identify a current task or project where it would be helpful to talk to the other person about what they should expect from you. What can you pull off? What's more of a stretch than you're up for?

- Make a point of noticing all the ways (big and small) that you work to stay on top of your ADHD. Write out a long list if that would make it more real. Maybe ask your family and friends for ideas if you need them. Take a moment to really appreciate everything you do.

• What, When, Where, and Why?

What strategies are you going to apply from this chapter? How will this be different from what you're already doing? Or perhaps have done before?

When and where? The more specific you can be, the better. Then actively look for these moments. Or set an alarm or other reminder to pull your attention to it. How can you set things up beforehand to make this easier to stick with?

Why? What problem will this solve or improve? What are all the direct and indirect benefits of this change? How is your life better for it? This is your motivation for when you don't feel like it.

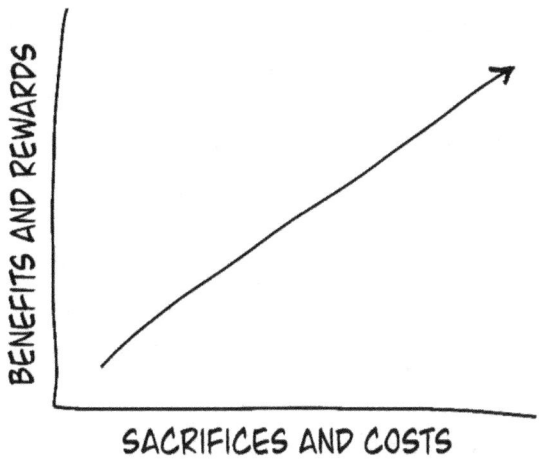

32. How Productive Do You Really Need to Be?

BEING MORE PRODUCTIVE IS A worthy goal for most people. Obviously. (Take a moment to silently mouth "duh.") Some people may have more ground to cover than others, but because life keeps evolving, none of us have the luxury of complacency. Besides all the tangible benefits of getting more done, there are also the emotional benefits of feeling better about yourself, of feeling less self-conscious whenever you occasionally drop the ball (or worry constantly that you have or will).

So, yes, definitely, let's aspire to be more productive. Sign me up. But here's the problem: nothing is free. Being more productive takes time and effort, both of which are finite resources. At some point, being a little bit more productive is not worth it. There's no benefit in growing more roses if you don't have time to smell them. At some point, you need to be OK with a few weeds. It's all about balance.

Productivity serves the greater purpose of living a meaningful life. Part of this involves feeling happy in the life you're living rather than wishing for something you don't have—or assuming that the only way to be happier is to have it. My hope is that at this point in your deep dive on productivity that you've made some helpful changes and are reaping the rewards. This improved situation may give you some perspective on what it would take to make the next changes. Hopefully you can see a place where good enough can be good enough.

> What do you want? And what are you willing to do to get it?

The Good Enough Threshold

I've spent a lot of pages on ways to make objective changes to your life. But it's interesting that objective improvement and subjective happiness aren't directly related. Becoming 20% more productive doesn't necessarily make you 20% happier. It may only be 5%, or even 95%. It depends where you started and where you want to end up.

This is important because if you feel like you need to be 100% productive in order to be happy, then you should probably give up now since you won't get there. Same goes if, on the inverse, you feel like you need to be 0% ADHD (aka, super-human). Goals that feel impossible are de-motivating. Much better is a goal that may feel like a stretch, but is still possible—and actually worth the effort.

So, think about what you're trying to do here. It might be that never being late to work is too lofty, but also unnecessary. Instead, being less late, less often might be enough. Your boss might not give you the Early Bird Award, but they also won't write you up or give you that dirty look that you dread. Even if a new strategy or system only works half the time, it's still better than a quarter. And a quarter is still better than not using it at all.

The better you really understand your ADHD and all the ways that it affects you, plus all of your strengths, the more reasonable some optimism might feel. Also, and equally, it may help you accept that certain things will always be difficult for you and will take extra effort and diligence. Fine. We're all a mix of strengths and weaknesses.

How Much Should Others Get to Vote?

Everyone has opinions about everything, but who should be allowed to vote on your desired level of productivity? It depends. If your productivity has a direct impact on them, they may have stronger feelings about you stepping it up. If it's your boss, they have more decision-making power than you do, so they can certainly make their desires known and exert some consequences if they don't think you hit the mark. Ultimately, you retain the ability to end a relationship (i.e., remove their vote) with someone who treats you unfairly, but quitting a job or relationship may be too drastic a solution. In this case, you may prefer to do what you can to please them while reminding yourself that this is what's best for you under these circumstances and that that doesn't mean you endorse their opinion. Sometimes we need to go along to get along.

If you and the other person are more equal, like with a coworker, romantic partner, or friend, then you should be able to negotiate as equals. This means both people get equal votes on what you each do and how you do it. This makes for more negotiation than commands. Unfortunately, if dropping the ball too often has tarnished your credibility, the other person may feel that they need to be "the responsible one" and make sure that things get done. In other words, they get more votes. This might be fine if you're both cool with it—let's run with our strengths.

Where it gets messy is when both people aren't cool with it. You may bristle at being told what to do, especially with that tone (you know which tone). And even though the other person designated themselves the unofficial boss, they may not actually want the job. Mostly what they want is to not worry about things getting done, so taking charge is the means to that end. This might be great for productivity but may sacrifice the relationship in the process—not fun at work and not sexy at home. The other person may not feel great about it, and being told what to do isn't going to build up your self-esteem either. What's worse, if you feel like you aren't managing your ADHD well, you may secretly agree that you deserve to be treated like the subordinate and that you shouldn't push to be equals because you doubt you could hold up your end of the bargain. This is the ultimate interpersonal price of ADHD.

People-Pleasing Won't Please You

We're social creatures. Other people's opinions of us can carry some real consequences, so we should pay attention to what people think. Equally, we need to know our own truth, accept that others won't always know the whole story, and recognize that everyone has biases. If you spent a bunch of years with undiagnosed ADHD, you may have internalized other people's judgments of you and, therefore, work really hard to make sure you don't disappoint anyone. (This is especially likely for women, given how girls are socialized.) In other words, if you buy into the idea that you "should just be normal like everyone else," then all these negative experiences teach you to give other people too much of a vote in how you feel about yourself. This can make for a lot of extra work and a lot more bad feelings. If you pin too much of your self-esteem to what other people think about you, it will sometimes push you to do things that aren't in your best interests. Or, based on the premise that you "just need to work harder," grind yourself down by working too hard to make sure something gets done. (Spoiler alert: working harder is not a cure for ADHD.) All of this will give some unscrupulous or needy folks too much influence over your life.

> People-pleasing is a good idea taken too far.

It's OK to disappoint people sometimes, but there's a difference between making a decision to not do something versus dropping the ball. If you do too much of the latter, you may feel like you then can't stand your ground when you make a real choice. You've used up your free passes. One more disappointment may be the straw that breaks the camel's back.

This brings up the question of whose job it is to fix someone else's disappointment. You may choose to take on the responsibility to complete the task that they would like done. Maybe you also feel this task is important. Or maybe you're just being generous. This might be a good idea if the other person is generous with you or their opinion of you has some tangible effects. But maybe you don't want to or can't do the task, at least not without paying an unacceptable price. Maybe then the other person needs to find a way to be OK with the task not being done, at least not by you or perhaps not now. Maybe this is more of their problem, and you don't have to be the solution.

I'm all in favor of being a good team player. There are benefits that come from collaboration. Everyone should carry their weight. This might mean that you need to step up to do what is being expected of you, but it may also mean that you know when to hold the line on not doing something and find a way to be OK with the other person's feelings about it. This is a book about productivity, not productivity at all costs.

Put It to Work

- Identify where your ideas of productivity come from. What do they tell you about yourself? What do they tell you about ADHD? Do these ideas still serve you well?

- Identify a goal where good enough is good enough. How can you help yourself feel OK about that? How can you handle others perhaps having different expectations for what's good enough?

- Identify a situation where you're doing something for someone else and it might be helpful to talk to them about their expectations for you. What would you want to know from them? What would you want them to know about you? How much is their disappointment your job to fix?

- ## What, When, Where, and Why?

What strategies are you going to apply from this chapter? How will this be different from what you're already doing? Or perhaps have done before?

When and where? The more specific you can be, the better. Then actively look for these moments. Or set an alarm or other reminder to pull your attention to it. How can you set things up beforehand to make this easier to stick with?

Why? What problem will this solve or improve? What are all the direct and indirect benefits of this change? How is your life better for it? This is your motivation for when you don't feel like it.

33. Should You Tell People You Have ADHD?

THERE IS NOTHING WRONG WITH having ADHD. Let's say that again: There is nothing wrong with having ADHD.

This question of to tell or not to tell in no way implies that having ADHD is a dark secret or something to feel bad about. Having ADHD means that you have at least some of a bunch of genes that are mostly involved with dopamine receptors, so you apply your executive functions less consistently. That's it. Everything else that you think or feel about ADHD depends on how it shows up in your life and the interpretations that you and others make about it. This brings up a point we'll get to in a minute—the choice to disclose personal information also depends on who you're disclosing it to.

Personal information, of all sorts, is private. We can choose to disclose it, but we have no obligation to do so, even if someone asks. If someone asked you your favorite sexual fantasies or greatest fears, would you automatically tell them? The hope for sharing personal information is that we do it in a well thought out way that we still feel good about afterwards. By contrast, a blurted-out disclosure or one that comes out of insecurity, with probably too many apologies or too much defensiveness, only make messy situations messier. You may tell too much, not enough, or in a way that gives the wrong impression.

A wise disclosure takes the time to understand and integrate what ADHD means to you before sharing with others. Not that you have to have it all figured out, since that understanding will likely evolve as you continue to learn more about ADHD and about yourself overall.

You may also want to think about why you're sharing this information. What are you hoping to accomplish? How likely is it to work out that way? Is there another way to accomplish the same thing without sharing what can't be unshared?

Treatment Can Delay Disclosure

Hopefully we use our words to share something about ourselves, but because other people have eyes and ears, they pick up a lot on their own. Unfortunately, if you're not managing your ADHD well, then other people will see it in various ways. They will start making assumptions about why you do what you do and what it means about you. In their defense, we all make these inferences about other people. It's part of what allows society to function without every single person needing to explain every single thing they do—could you imagine how boring that would be? Mostly this process of making assumptions works well enough, except when it doesn't.

There is some personal information that is less visible to others, which gives you the luxury of disclosing on your own schedule—or never. Since ADHD can be so visible, it affects how you interact with other people and the assumptions

> "ADHD is the worst kept secret."
> Stephanie Sarkis, PhD

they make about you. If you don't like those assumptions (or what you assume they're assuming), then it can feel like it paints you into a corner of having to disclose because disclosure is less terrible than being judged unfairly. It's easy for someone to look at a pattern of behavior and make assumptions about not only your intentions, but even your character. Yikes. In this case, silence is anything but golden.

Despair not! You have a number of options to avoid being painted with the irresponsible jerk brush. One obvious way is to make your ADHD less visible to others. Whether it's medication, therapy, coaching, hiring an organizer, or scribbling strategies from this book all over your arms, the better you manage your ADHD, the more secret it becomes. In other words, you can choose to disclose it—or not. You don't even need to become super-human; just close enough to good enough. This converts symptoms into colorful quirks or rounding errors. Or round enough errors.

Getting more on top of your ADHD, and thereby your responsibilities, also puts you in a stronger position with other people. I think we should all be able to ask for some forgiveness and benefit of the doubt, but most people have a limit to their generosity. If you ask others to work harder at overlooking and compensating for your ADHD moments than you do at preventing them, that relationship will have problems. Managing your ADHD more effectively might give you less to have to explain and then hope for a decent response.

Disclosure Depends on Both People

Disclosure happens between two people, so your decision will depend on how you feel about your ADHD and about yourself overall, as well as on how you feel about the other person. The more secure you are in yourself, in general and specifically about your ADHD, the more confident you may feel to share something because you can tolerate the other person having a response that's less than what you would hope for. Obviously, it also depends on whether the other person can tangibly affect your life, like with a boss. We will cover the additional practical and legal considerations of disclosing at work in the next chapter, but this may also be relevant for other situations, such as when someone has a lot of influence in your friend group.

The other half of your mental math on disclosing is the other person's perceived trustworthiness (i.e., their worthiness of trust). Is this someone who generally handles personal information well? If they tend to gossip and share other people's secrets, then they're more likely to share yours. You also want to consider how empathetic versus judgmental they are on mental health issues, general human fallibility, and people who are different from them.

It's worth reminding yourself that if someone responds badly to a disclosure, or if you're worried that they might, that may tell you more about them than it

> You can't punish honesty and expect the truth.

does about what you're disclosing. Maybe this is a blind spot for them or something that tweaks their issues. For example, someone who is really critical probably has trouble accepting their own faults and perhaps grew up with a lot of criticism themselves. Knowing this might give me a little compassion for them, but I still wouldn't share much.

You might also find yourself in a situation where the person that you're considering disclosing to is overly invested in a particular narrative about you and isn't really interested in updating their perspective. For example, a friend who needs to feel superior to mask their own insecurity needs you to be the one who messes up. Or someone who likes to play the victim needs to feel justified in their mistreatment, which just won't feel the same if you have your own struggles. Someone who is fixed in their narratives tends to be difficult to be close with because there isn't enough room for who the other person really is.

Having said all that, I'm totally OK with someone not knowing anything or having some inaccurate ideas about ADHD or whatever you might disclose. Ignorance is completely acceptable, as long as it's accompanied by more curiosity than judgment or rigidity. You might need to be the one to educate them on both what it means to have ADHD and also what it doesn't.

A Better Way

Sometimes all this "Should I? Shouldn't I?" is too much work. Or you just don't want to go there with this person at this time. My advice here is to talk symptoms before diagnoses. As in, just say, "I have trouble remembering to do things later." Leave out the part about ADHD and get right to how it affects what you do. This avoids the potential complications that might come from them having some inaccurate ideas about ADHD. While it is important for members of misunderstood groups to be out because it reduces stigma, you're not morally obligated to always be out. Sometimes you just want a quiet day.

You may be hesitant to disclose even a symptom of ADHD. I get it that this can feel risky, at least with some people in some situations. Keep in mind here that this probably isn't a big secret anyway, or at least it probably won't be a secret for much longer, so you're not losing much by putting this out there. By being direct about saying it, you may even get points for self-awareness and honesty. This also gives you an opportunity to explain a bit more about it and to help the other person understand it rather than letting them jump to their own conclusions about it. As they say in politics, get ahead of the story. By starting with a smaller disclosure, it lets you test out how the other person responds. Ball's in their court as to whether they get told more.

> Talk symptoms before diagnoses.
> It defers the bigger disclosure.

You may want to think about what types of questions or comments you might get and how you would answer them—and how you wouldn't. Simple, non-defensive answers spoken directly and calmly tend to evoke more acceptance and fewer challenging reactions. If someone continues to push more than you would like, just keep coming back to your original answers. Finally, if they're really not catching a clue, you can simply state that you don't want to talk more about it and that you don't want more questions.

The next chapter covers even more strategies for how to use disclosures wisely, mostly at work.

Put It to Work

- Reflect on how you feel about having ADHD and how that might impact how you would disclose it to others. What thoughts or feelings might unintentionally leak out?

- Think about why you have or haven't disclosed your ADHD and to who. How did those work out? What would you do differently? Would some wise disclosures now be helpful?

- Craft some language you can use to talk symptoms before diagnoses for when you might need it. What would you want to say—and not say? Practice saying it out loud so you have it down cold for when you might be nervous.

- ## What, When, Where, and Why?

  What strategies are you going to apply from this chapter? How will this be different from what you're already doing? Or perhaps have done before?

  When and where? The more specific you can be, the better. Then actively look for these moments. Or set an alarm or other reminder to pull your attention to it. How can you set things up beforehand to make this easier to stick with?

  Why? What problem will this solve or improve? What are all the direct and indirect benefits of this change? How is your life better for it? This is your motivation for when you don't feel like it.

34. What About Disclosing at Work?

WHEN IT COMES TO DISCLOSURES, the workplace is more complicated because there are laws and possibly company policies that impact how disclosures need to be handled. Certain revelations, even when said in passing, can prompt managers to make an anxious call to human resources to find out what they need to do. This might then prompt a call to you from HR. The positive spin on this is that it is in the interest of ensuring a fair process and that you are given the protections that you're due. The bad news is that it might involve meetings, paperwork, and extra monitoring and documentation. How this all gets handled will depend a lot on your manager and also on the general culture of your employer—as much as there are official requirements, there's always some room to lean things one way or the other. You may want to think about what kind of a reception you might get before disclosing anything "interesting."

It's also worth noting here that the protections and accommodations that you may have received in school are very different from what you can expect in the workplace. Obviously, any employer can choose to offer extensive supports, but the mandated accommodations are much less. Again, this doesn't mean that you shouldn't ask for accommodations, but it's helpful to know what you're walking into.

> Remember, HR's job is to protect the company, not necessarily to protect you.

Ask for What You Need

Everyone has their individual strengths, weaknesses, quirks, and preferences. ADHD might influence some of this for you but also there is the rest of your personality and who you are. Same for your co-workers who are a mix of traits and preferences. Every employee will have an easier time with some aspects of the job and struggle more with others. So if there are some reasonable steps your employer or co-workers can take that would make you a better employee, then ask for those accommodations. Don't feel bad or minimize where you're struggling—it's probably not much of a secret anyway. And definitely don't over-apologize—this can make the other person uncomfortable if they feel like it's now their job to make sure you feel OK.

Be specific in what you're asking for and then explain how the other person stands to benefit too. For example, saying, "That's a lot of details. Can I email you a list to make sure I got it all?" Or, "Can I come in early or stay late so I can really focus on that complicated project when it's quieter?." Most people will have an easy time saying yes to requests like these. Plus, they will see you as a diligent problem-solver.

Offer Permission

Don't assume that other people will know how to respond to ADHD-related situations, like if you forget to call someone back. It's easy for them to start making assumptions—she's too busy, this isn't important to her, she doesn't care about keeping me waiting, etc. You may need to offer them permission to do something that they wouldn't otherwise do that will make them happier (and make it easier for you to be a good employee). For example, you could say, "I try really hard, but I'm not always great at calling back, so feel free to bug me."

Now, some people might say that it isn't their job to be your executive assistant. Agreed. But it is their job to do what will make *them* happier. If a quick call or text gets them the information they were waiting for, then that seems like a good use of effort compared to resentfully waiting. Also, by giving permission for them to reach out, you're showing that it's important to you to do a good job, something that ADHD can undermine by making them think you don't care.

A Wise Disclosure

Before disclosing your ADHD, whether officially or in passing, make an honest assessment of your boss and company's likely response. How do they tend to handle situations that go beyond the standard procedures? How much do they value employee satisfaction (a.k.a., retention) versus brute efficiency? This is one of those situations where you may be right, but not happy, if they punish your disclosure. They probably won't be so bold as to just fire you on the spot, and they certainly won't write ADHD as the reason for termination, but you may find that their attitude towards you has shifted, that they're paying more attention to your every action and maybe even writing it down. Or maybe the better assignments start going to a colleague.

This is one of those situations where you might be happier accepting the hard truth that this isn't going to get better and see if you can find a way to accept this job for what it is and be happy enough with it. Alternatively, you may come around to the idea that this job just isn't a good fit and decide to seek greener pastures elsewhere. Sometimes the job itself is fine, but the problem is the fit with coworkers or management. Getting the same job elsewhere or even in a different department might work out better. Obviously, changing jobs can be a really big production—I don't want to pretend it isn't. In the end, though, it may be better than trying to force a bad situation into being good. And it's always better to leave with a clean record, by your own choice, and on your own timing than to be pushed out.

Do Accommodations Right

If you're going to disclose your ADHD and possibly ask for accommodations, it's always better to do so while good will remains. If you're on a performance improvement plan or on the verge of one, your boss will probably be much less receptive and see it as a way to pull your bacon out of the fire. At a minimum, they may be annoyed that you hadn't let them know earlier, before they filled out all that paperwork. Plus, because HR is covering their bases against a potential lawsuit, it might now be hard to get that train off the track.

Regardless of when or how you disclosed your ADHD, you need to show your boss that this is in the pursuit of being a more effective employee. That's a sales pitch that will convince most bosses. You can ask for accommodations if you think they will help, but the greater burden of effort is on you to earn your keep.

In this process, you may need to educate your manager, coworkers, and/or HR about ADHD in general, but mostly you need to explain how it affects you—and also how it doesn't, just in case they have any crazy ideas. It might be helpful to include some brief selected readings or recordings to lend credibility or to explain something better than you could. Make the information specific to your situation and pointed towards possible solutions. And probably shorter than you think it should be.

> Find a work situation that's a good fit. Then work hard to make it great.

If you're looking for guidance on accommodations of all kinds, www.askJAN.org is a federally funded, free program that is a treasure trove for employees, employers, and policy makers. You can even talk to one of their advisors.

Put It to Work

- Have you considered disclosing ADHD at work? What factors went into the decision? What do you know about your company's culture? What leans you towards yes and what leans you away?

- Reflect on your boss and colleagues—what about them suggests they would respond well? Or poorly? How have other disclosures of various kinds by you or other people been received?

- What specific requests or accommodations would make you a more effective employee? What could you tell your boss to possibly convince them? What would their resistance be and how could you counter that?

- ## What, When, Where, and Why?

  What strategies are you going to apply from this chapter? How will this be different from what you're already doing? Or perhaps have done before?

  When and where? The more specific you can be, the better. Then actively look for these moments. Or set an alarm or other reminder to pull your attention to it. How can you set things up beforehand to make this easier to stick with?

  Why? What problem will this solve or improve? What are all the direct and indirect benefits of this change? How is your life better for it? This is your motivation for when you don't feel like it.

35. Disappoint and Disagree with Grace

WE ALL HOPE THAT WE will do a good job on our various responsibilities and that other people will be happy with us. Sure, when everything goes according to plan. Assuming there was a plan. But what about when things go sideways? It happens to all of us.

When it comes to delivering bad news, here's my really strong advice: Disappoint early. Just bite the bullet and do it. No waiting for the perfect moment or telling yourself why this isn't a good time.

Sure, that's yet another awesome recommendation on that giant pile of Things That Are Easy to Say and Really Hard to Do. So, let's break this down to make it a bit easier—not easy, but easier.

As we all know, the longer we wait to deliver bad news, the worse it gets. Not only does delivering bad news at the last minute give the other person less time to adjust, it also makes one problem (not doing what they were expecting) into two problems (now they have a last minute crisis). Sometimes that second one is actually worse than the first.

Unfortunately, ADHD can be a double whammy where it's easy to over-promise and also easy to under-deliver. And to procrastinate, so you don't even know that you're going to miss the mark until it's too late.

ADHD aside, no one is 100% reliable. We all need to be able to tell someone that we aren't going to do what we agreed to do. Things come up that we couldn't have predicted and can't control, like a more important meeting gets called or someone gets sick. The problem is that if you tend to be less reliable than average, you use up your free passes too quickly, and the other person may be less forgiving (or believing) when these other situations come up. Or you may feel overly self-conscious asking for a pass even when the problem isn't in your control. Or you will somehow find a way to give yourself at least some of the blame anyway.

There's also the situation where you still could do the task, but you changed your mind and just don't want to. As a free agent, you made the decision to spend your time in other ways. This is completely different from dropping the ball where you allowed the situation to spin out of your control. Again, a history of ADHD-related falling short can make it feel like you don't have the right to change your mind.

For all of these reasons, it's important to improve your batting average (like with all the strategies in this book and elsewhere). This will reduce the number of situations where you don't follow through, which has obvious social benefits. This greater consistency then gives you greater standing to choose something different from the other person's expectations, which means you will hit the mark more for what you do take on. Also, you can pump up your batting average, not just by hitting more, but also by only swinging at the good ones.

Avoid False Agreements

A false agreement is a situation where someone lets the other person think that they agree when they actually don't. Obviously, this tends to cause big trouble later when the truth comes out, especially if the other person sees the false agreement as an outright lie or a lie of omission (knowingly withholding the truth) based in some selfish or nefarious intent. This may not be what's in your heart, but it's a problem if it looks that way to the other person, or if they decide that that's the deal. I say that ADHD is a disorder of converting intentions reliably into actions, so if someone reverse engineers your intentions based on your actions (or inactions), then you have some damage control to do. For example, if someone assumes you don't value their time if you tend to run late.

False agreements can come about in two ways. The first involves how carefully you think before you agree to the task. If you agree before pausing to really think about whether you can or want to take on the task, your agreement is more of a kneejerk response than a real commitment. The intentions are good, but not fully thought out. Technically this isn't a false agreement, but it will probably look like one to the other person, so you have the same social fallout.

These impulsive yeses are fine for some things, unless the other person now thinks that you're totally in—maybe not with a blood oath, but with a pretty solid *yep!* They're counting on you, but you haven't fully thought through whether it's possible to fulfill the agreement. In theory, there may be time for everything; in reality, a lot of that time has already been spoken for, or will be (like with all the other stuff you need to do), so it may not actually be possible for you to complete the requested task on time.

The ADHD bonus points on this is impulsively agreeing because you are a good person and want to be helpful, but didn't pause to really think about the time commitment and potential conflicts. Before committing, you might need to check your schedule and to do list. Which, of course, assumes that they're filled in (*Yep, totally blank. I got plenty of time!*). Or you might need to check something and get back to them, which involves needing to remember (fingers crossed!), so instead of rolling those dice, you just agree now. If all this sounds painfully familiar, you may want to go back to *Section V. Sharpen Your Tools.*

Of course, just because you have the time doesn't mean that you want to spend it on what is being asked of you. Again, recognizing this involves pausing long enough to get clear on how you feel about it and whether it makes the cut. If you agree too quickly now, you will probably regret it later, which will make it really hard to motivate for, which will just supercharge your procrastination.

The second way that false agreements get set up is more about emotional tolerance. In this case, you have decided that you don't want to agree to the requested task, but you worry about the other person's reaction. If you have a conscience, you don't enjoy disappointing people. That discomfort is pretty universal. Depending on how conflict was handled in your family, you may feel really uncomfortable or like you don't have the right to disappoint others, so you will avoid it if you can. A lifetime of ADHD disappointing may also have taught you to just agree and suck it up, especially if you are female and were socialized to be accommodating.

> Trust is based in predictability and transparency.
> If you sometimes struggle with the first one, then it's really important to be good at the second.

Of course, your comfort in saying no also depends on how you expect the other person to respond—someone who freaks out, blows up, plays the guilt card, or falls apart will punish honesty, so it's even harder to tell these people the truth. These folks will require some varsity-level assertiveness skills. It's really tempting to just yes them in the moment and then later regret the corner you've painted yourself into. With folks like these, you may want to seriously consider whether this is someone who should play a smaller role in your life. And certainly you shouldn't take their bad behavior personally—that reflects on them, not you. Being occasionally disappointed or frustrated is to be expected in life, but it doesn't grant anyone carte blanche to respond however they want—or require you to be OK with their behavior.

Assuming the other person's reaction is proportional to the level of disappointment, then the ball is in your court to handle the feelings that it brings up in you. This might begin with reminding yourself that you have the right to not do what someone wants from you. You have the right to say no—and to still feel OK about yourself. Even if you mess things up more often than the other person does, that doesn't obligate you to always play catch up with them.

If you find yourself too often avoiding even minor conflict or agreeing to requests against your better judgment and then praying for a miracle, you may find it helpful to talk to a therapist about assertiveness and conflict management skills. These are relationship muscles that you can strengthen and that will make your life much easier.

> Someone else's negative emotions don't need to hijack yours.

Learn to Cut Things Loose

The obvious part of productivity is getting more things done. The equally important but probably less obvious part is making good decisions about what you *won't* be doing. Preserving motivation and mental bandwidth for one task may involve passing on another task. Or lots of other tasks.

It's tempting to think that we can do it all because it spares us having to make some difficult decisions. This is especially true if you tend to underestimate the time necessary for the new task and also overestimate the time you have available—two universal tendencies that are exacerbated by ADHD. If your plate is already overloaded, you're in for trouble when someone else tries to add something new. It might look like you're bad at getting things done, but it's really that you're too good at adding tasks and therefore have too much to do. Working faster and cutting corners will only take you so far. You can work more hours to get it all done, but there are limits to this, too.

At this point, your only salvation is to pause and really think through what you're cutting loose. This tends to work out better than optimistically plowing through and then letting circumstances decide for you—which too often means that what gets cut loose is whatever isn't finished when you run out of time. It can take some real cognitive effort to sort through all your demands, and then some emotional effort to be OK with letting some things go, especially if letting go will disappoint someone else. Still, it's better to be an active decision-maker in your life than a passive recipient.

There's also perhaps the option of not taking on any new projects until you've cleared the backlog. Life doesn't always offer this option, but some variation of this could be helpful if it means you'll be able to get more things out than come in—as long as you don't need to live to three hundred to balance the equation.

Put ADHD in Its Place

You're in a much stronger bargaining position with other people when you have more successes and fewer failures. The hoped for forgiveness and/or flexibility is earned. This requires getting on top of your ADHD—not perfect, but pretty good. Insufficiently managed ADHD can make you the obvious culprit when wires get crossed or something didn't work out—as in, if there's any doubt, let's blame you because you're usually the one who messes things up. While statistically that might tend to be true, it's not *always* true or true this time—but you may still be presumed guilty until proven innocent. It may be hard to shake that rep even if you really have made changes. You may need to have some direct conversations and ask that people watch how you're doing these days and possibly update their impression of you.

Being more reliable also makes you more believable when the problem isn't about ADHD at all. As in, you didn't drop the ball, you just made a different decision or other circumstances came up that changed your mental math on what to do. This way, the change of plans doesn't feel like a cover-up for forgetting or procrastinating. Of course, you will still have your occasional ADHD moments, so owning up to it when it happens gives you even more credibility when you say that that isn't what happened here. You're more than just ADHD, so don't let it cast a shadow over everything else that you are.

Put It to Work

- Identify some recent examples of how some ADHD moments set you up to disappoint someone. Remember that feeling when trying to motivate yourself to manage the situation better next time.

- What can you tell yourself to help you hold your ground when you need to say no? What are you worried about? How likely is that to happen? How could you handle it if it did?

- How can you tell the difference between dropping the ball and changing your mind? (Hint: Does it feel like a task fell through the cracks or did you change your perspective?) How does this change how you handle the situations that come up?

• What, When, Where, and Why?

What strategies are you going to apply from this chapter? How will this be different from what you're already doing? Or perhaps have done before?

When and where? The more specific you can be, the better. Then actively look for these moments. Or set an alarm or other reminder to pull your attention to it. How can you set things up beforehand to make this easier to stick with?

Why? What problem will this solve or improve? What are all the direct and indirect benefits of this change? How is your life better for it? This is your motivation for when you don't feel like it.

CONCLUSION: BRING IT ALL TOGETHER

H OMESTRETCH, BABY!

36. You Deserve a Better Life

HOLY CRAP, YOU GOT ALL the way to the end of the book! And probably read at least some of the pages before this! This is a big deal. We covered a lot of ground. I asked you to really think about how you do all these various things and to try a bunch of new strategies. The reading was the easy part. Applying it in your life is the harder part, but that's always going to be true.

Let's take stock of what you've done since page 1.

What is most surprising to you about this whole process?

What are the most important changes in how you think about ADHD, productivity, yourself, or others' expectations?

Which new habits are most helpful to you?

Which new habits worked well but then dropped off, so it would be worthwhile to pick them up again?

What are the lessons learned from what didn't work out?

Which habits would be good to add in?

How is your life better now?

What bigger life goals now feel more possible?

I sincerely hope that you have some really big stuff in the answers above. And that you feel justifiably proud of it.

I also hope that your hard work taught you *a lot*:

- ADHD's impact on your productivity

- Which strategies work best for you

- More about yourself as a whole person

- How to navigate others' expectations

- What a good life looks like for you

All this talk of productivity is really just a means to an end. The *real* goal here is to live a good life, where you feel able to pursue what is important and meaningful to you. Where mostly you feel effective and can cut yourself some slack when you occasionally blow it. Where you feel connected to people in your life and can hold your head high. Where you can adapt smoothly as life evolves. Where you can bravely pursue new challenges.

Change takes effort. New habits are slippery. We need to fight the pull of the status quo, then continue pushing against inertia to keep that progress moving. When you get discouraged, remind yourself that there's a reason why all those therapists and coaches are busy all day—people are complicated and self-improvement is hard. Make a point of looking for those small changes that you're making along the way. You're probably really good at noticing when you mess up—and others are happy to point out if you somehow miss it. To give those new habits a fighting chance, you need to pile up the successes, including the small, incremental improvements. Don't let any of them slip by. Life doesn't get better with a lightning strike, but with a gradual dawn.

Remember, you don't need to become a fundamentally different person. The goal is to be you, but a little more on top of things. Real self-esteem doesn't require perfection. Real self-esteem can accept our flaws, weaknesses, and shortcomings without letting them overshadow what we like about ourselves. My hope is that, in all my pages about reducing the impact of ADHD on your life and improving productivity, you also found ways to feel better about all of who you are.

You are more than ADHD. It's a part of your life, but you don't want it to rule your life. The goal here is to reduce how often it trips you up so the best of who you are can shine through. Most of the time.

Just keep showing up.

Make today a good day, regardless of what happened yesterday.